Primal Consciousness

Coloring Book Therapy

Evolution Vol 1

Andrea Wood Schmitz

Published by Inkovator Publishing Company in 2015
First Edition, First Printing

ISBN-13: 978-1517317171

ISBN-10: 1517317177

Thank You

I praise you because I am fearfully and wonderfully made.

It is my understanding that we are created to create. We are created in the likeness of God!

Especially through difficult times in my life, creative outlets have allowed me to find peace. Painting, drawing and yes, coloring.

I am thankful to God for leading me during times of stress and creating me in His image.

I want to thank my husband, Peter. I appreciate you and the fact that you allow me the space to develop this series of coloring books. Without your support, they never would have reached this stage.

And I want to thank my co-conspirators in this series: Talita, Tiria, Simeon, Esra, Yael and Eaden. Your support and excitement made it worth the struggle an your input was invaluable. Thank you for the many years of coloring and may we have many more in the days to come!

Use this page as your
Color Test Page
For your markers, pencils and crayons

Place a piece of paper UNDERNEATH this page to test if your markers bleed through!

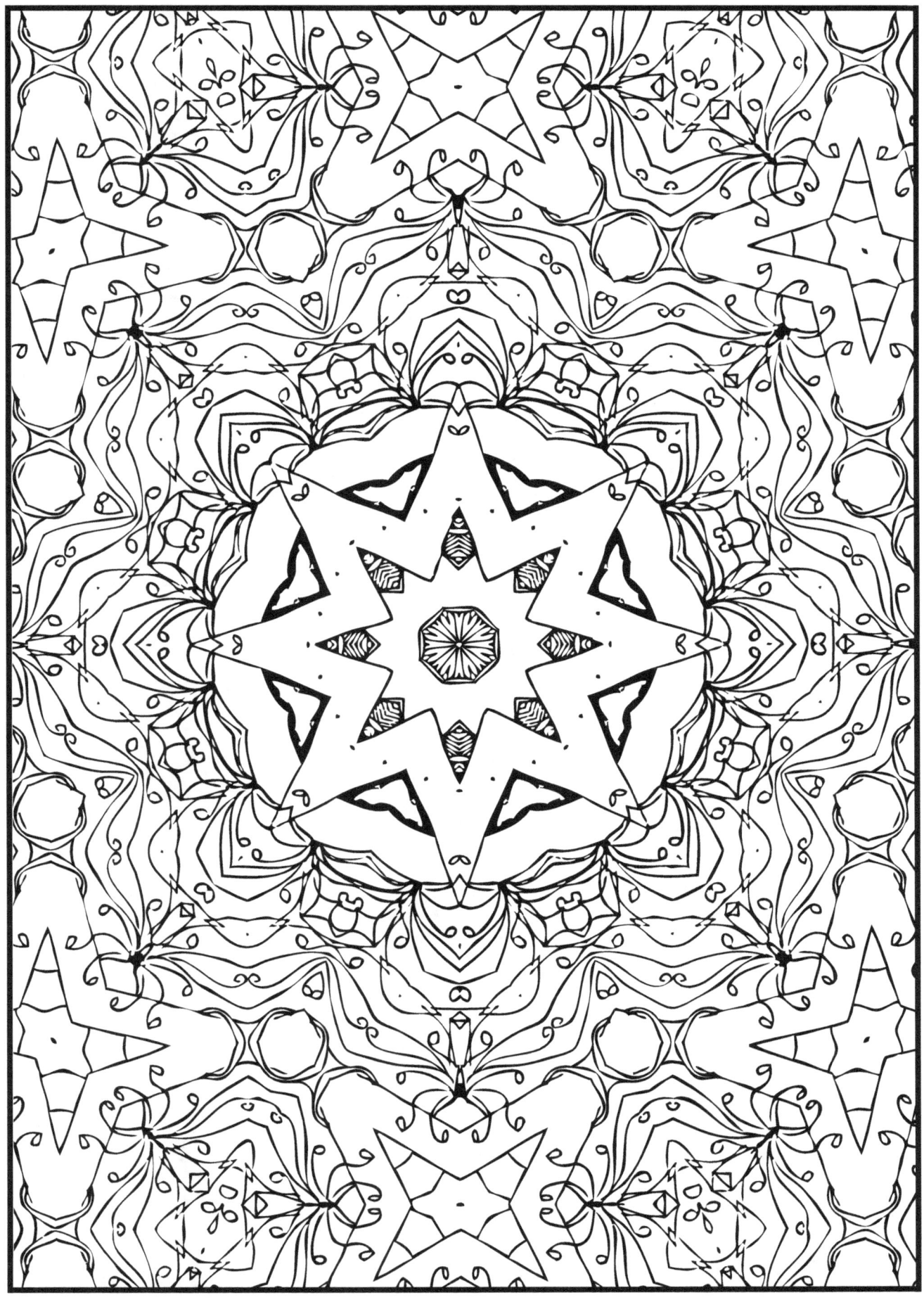

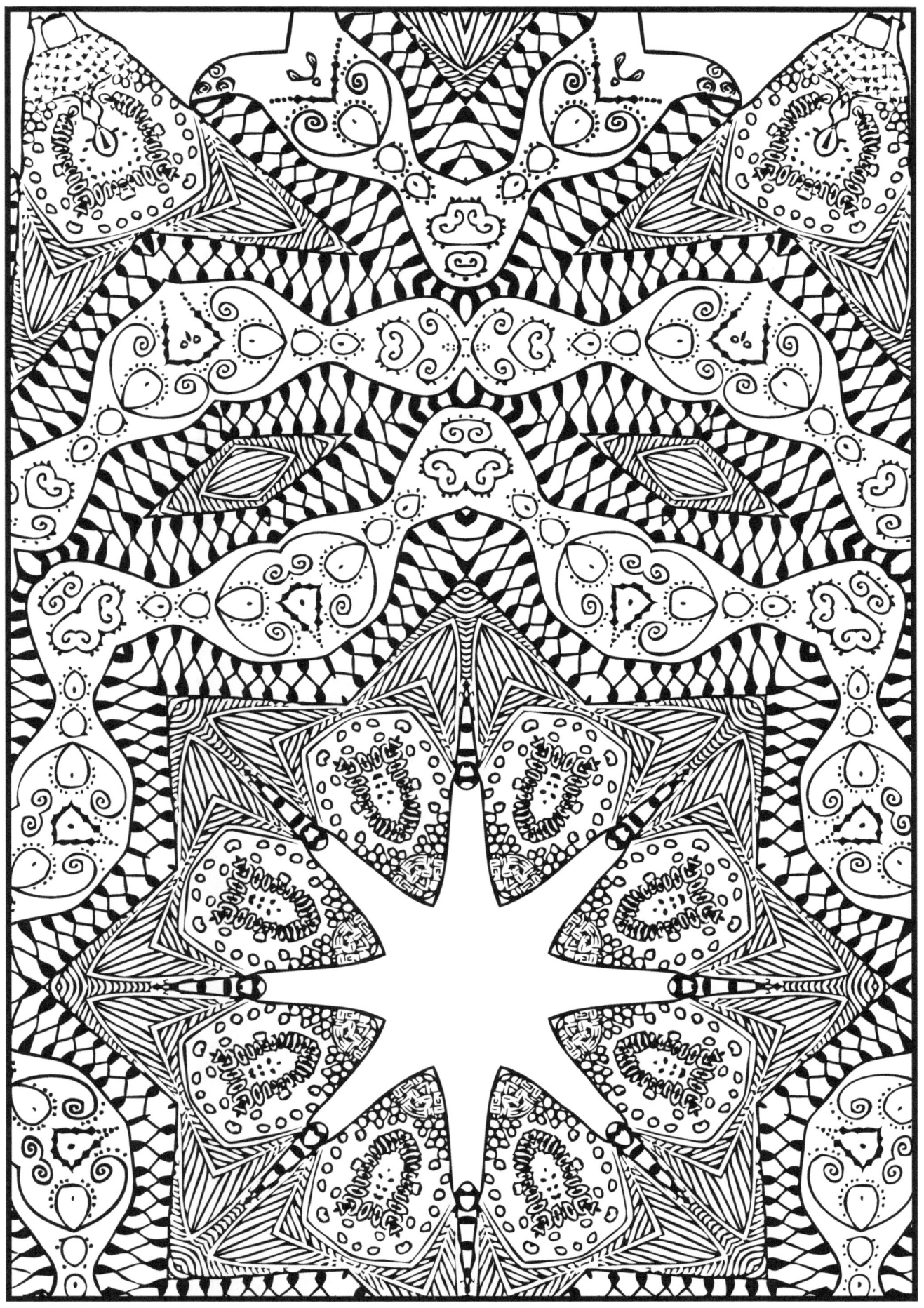

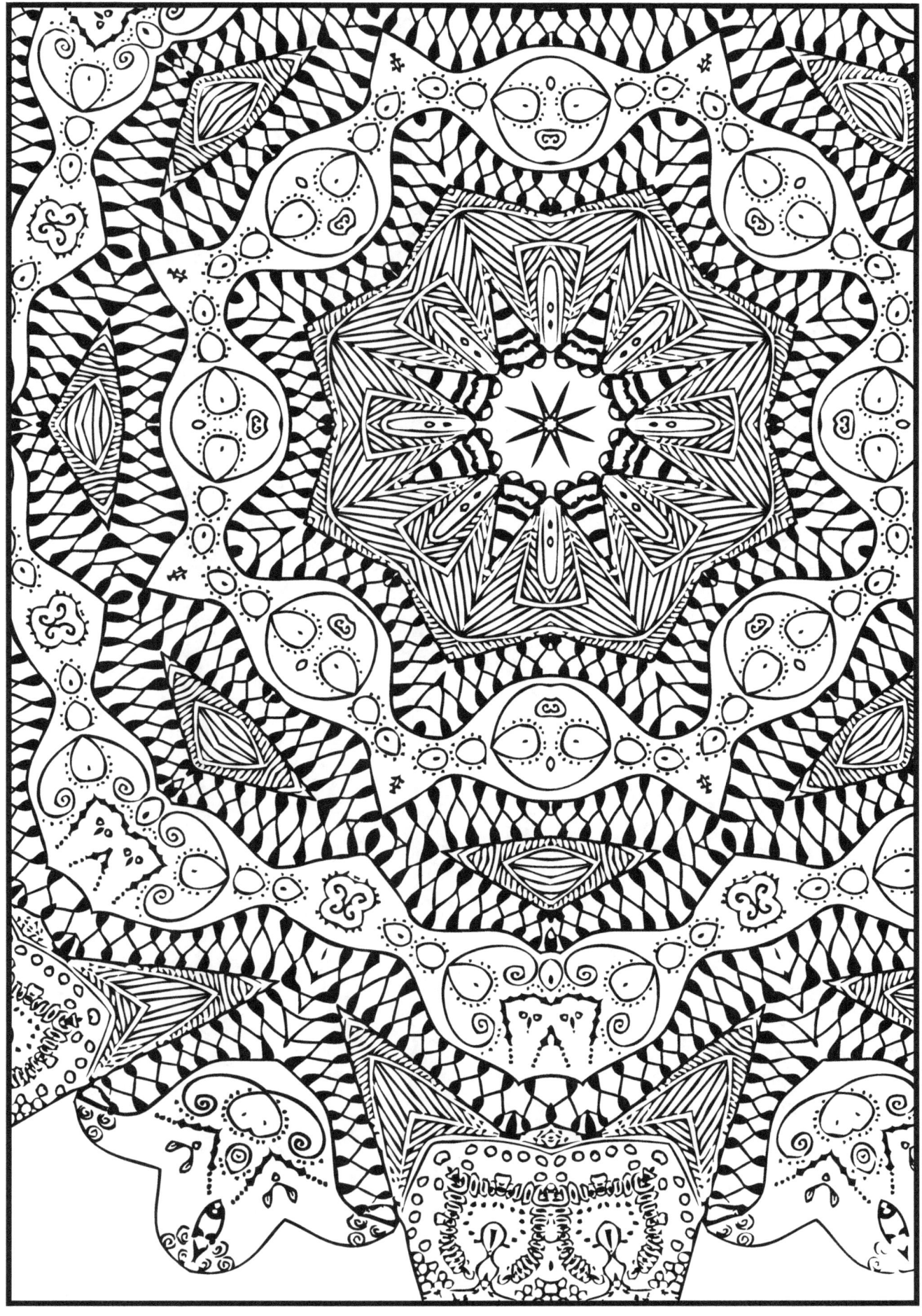

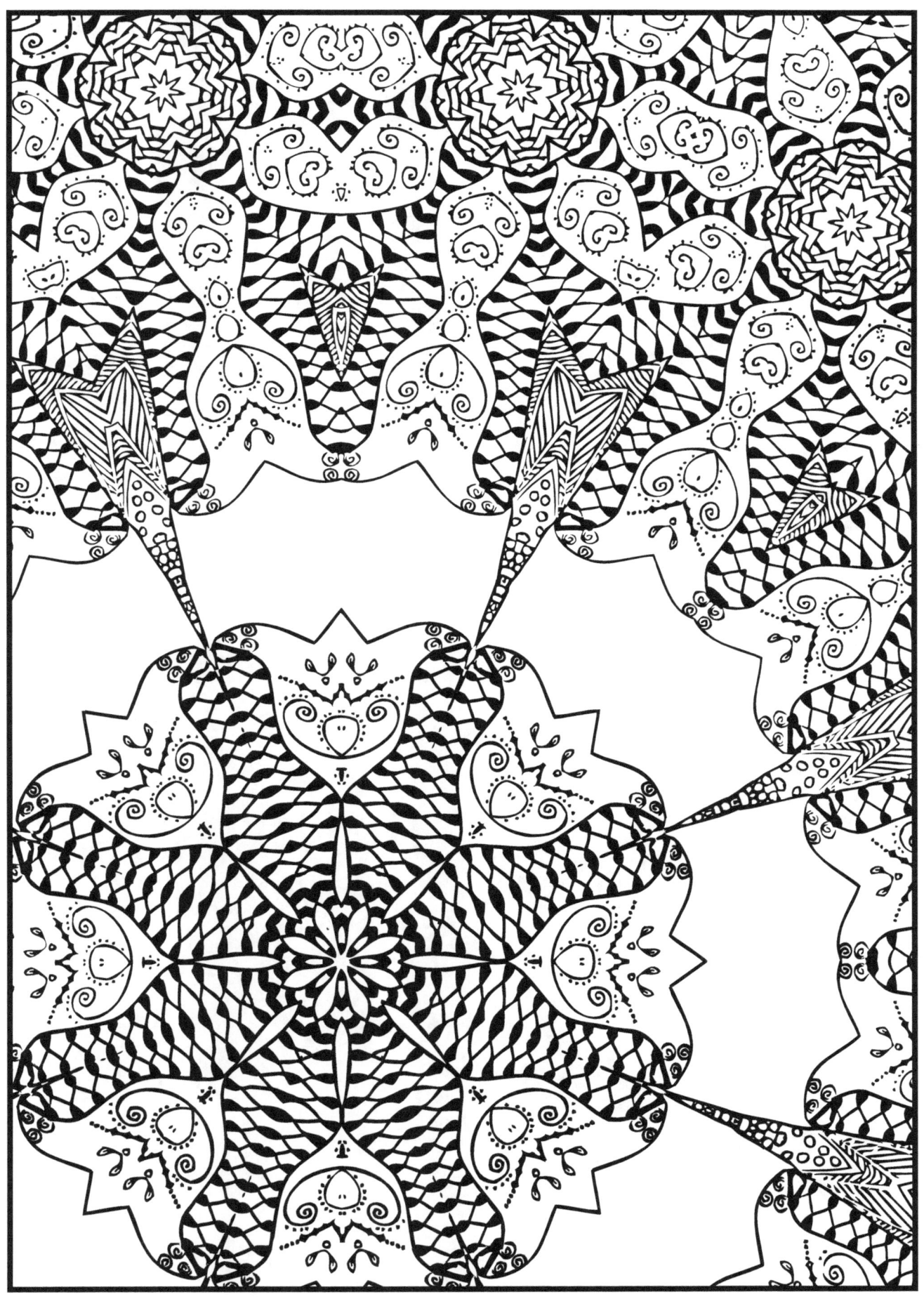

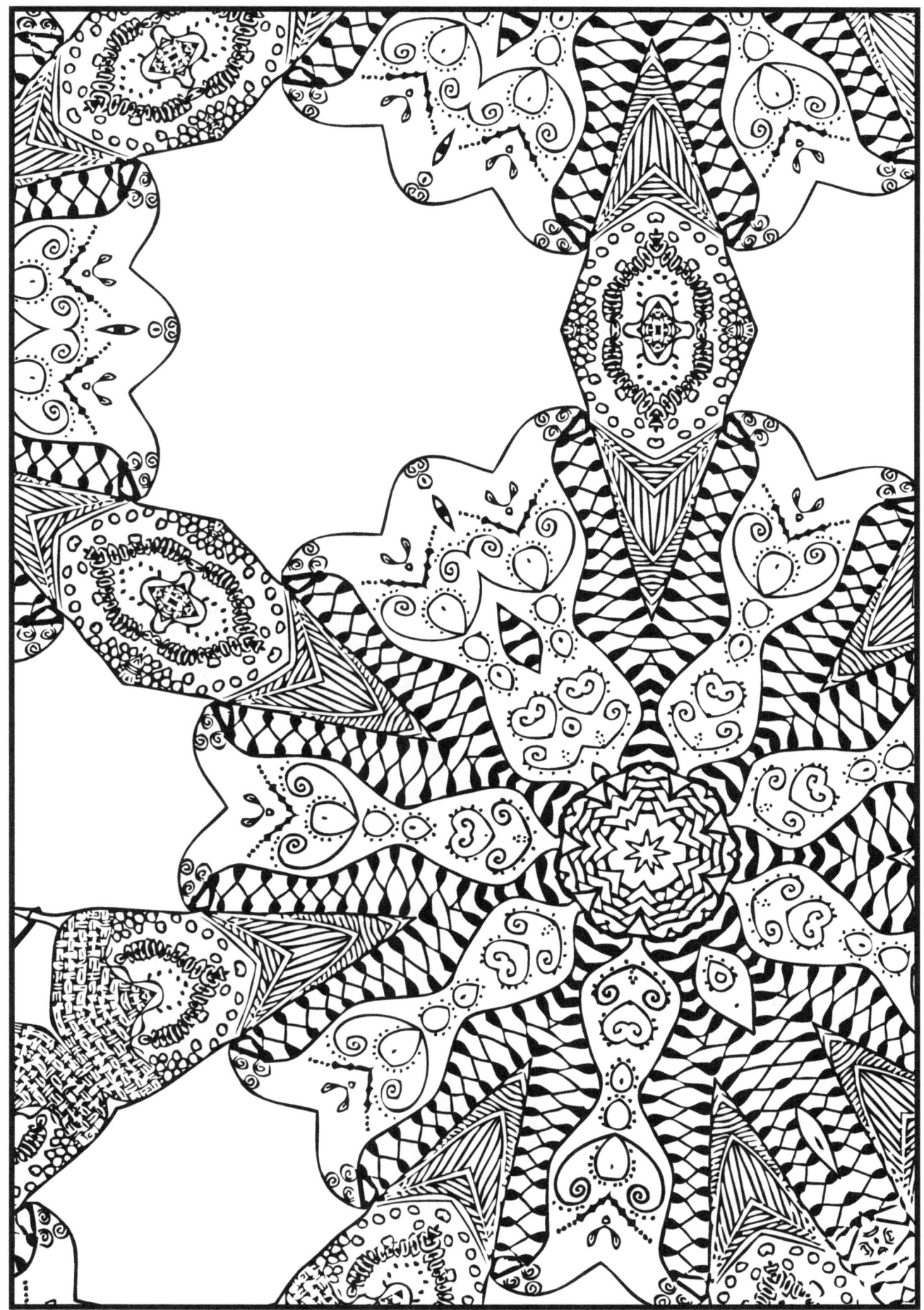

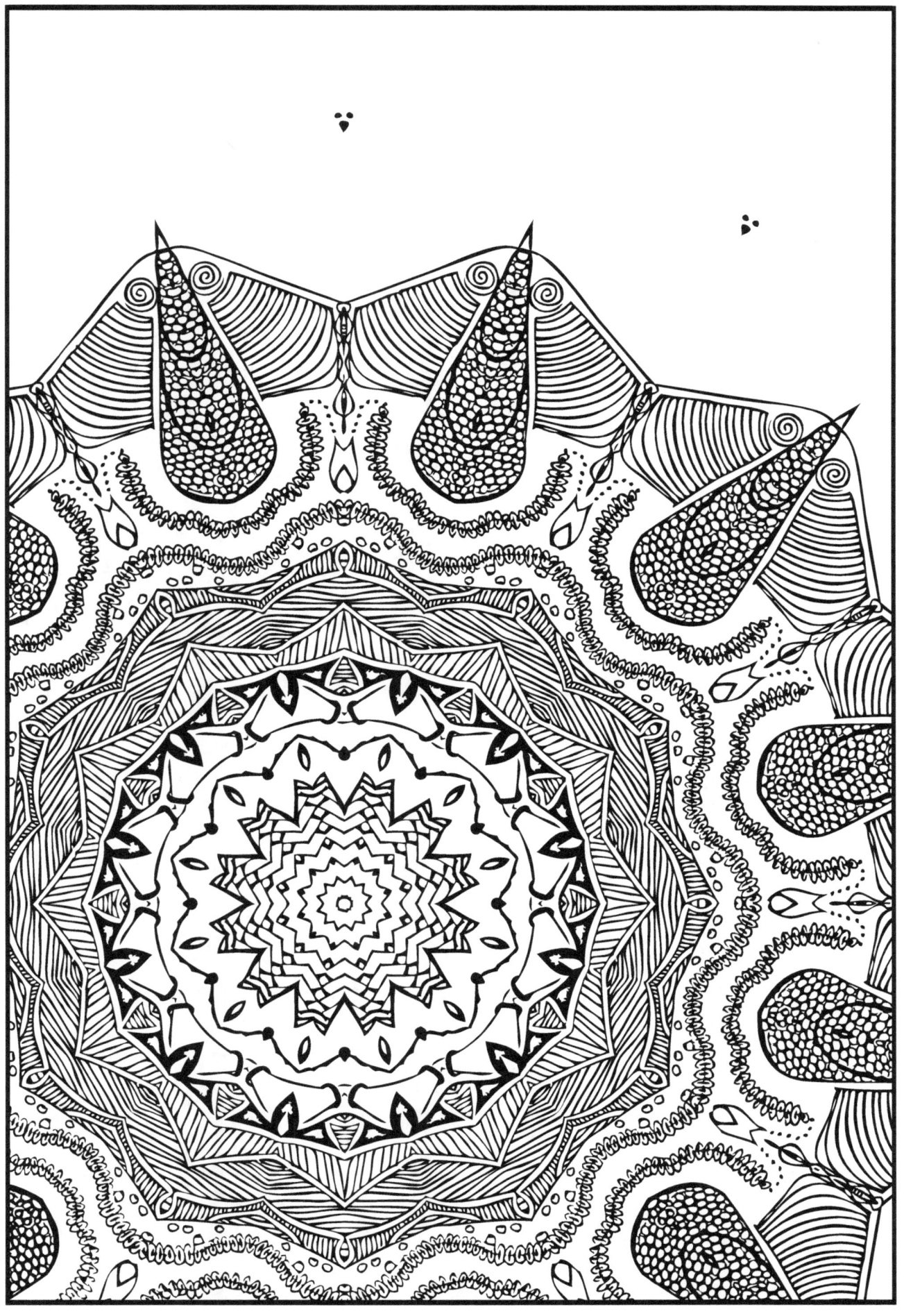

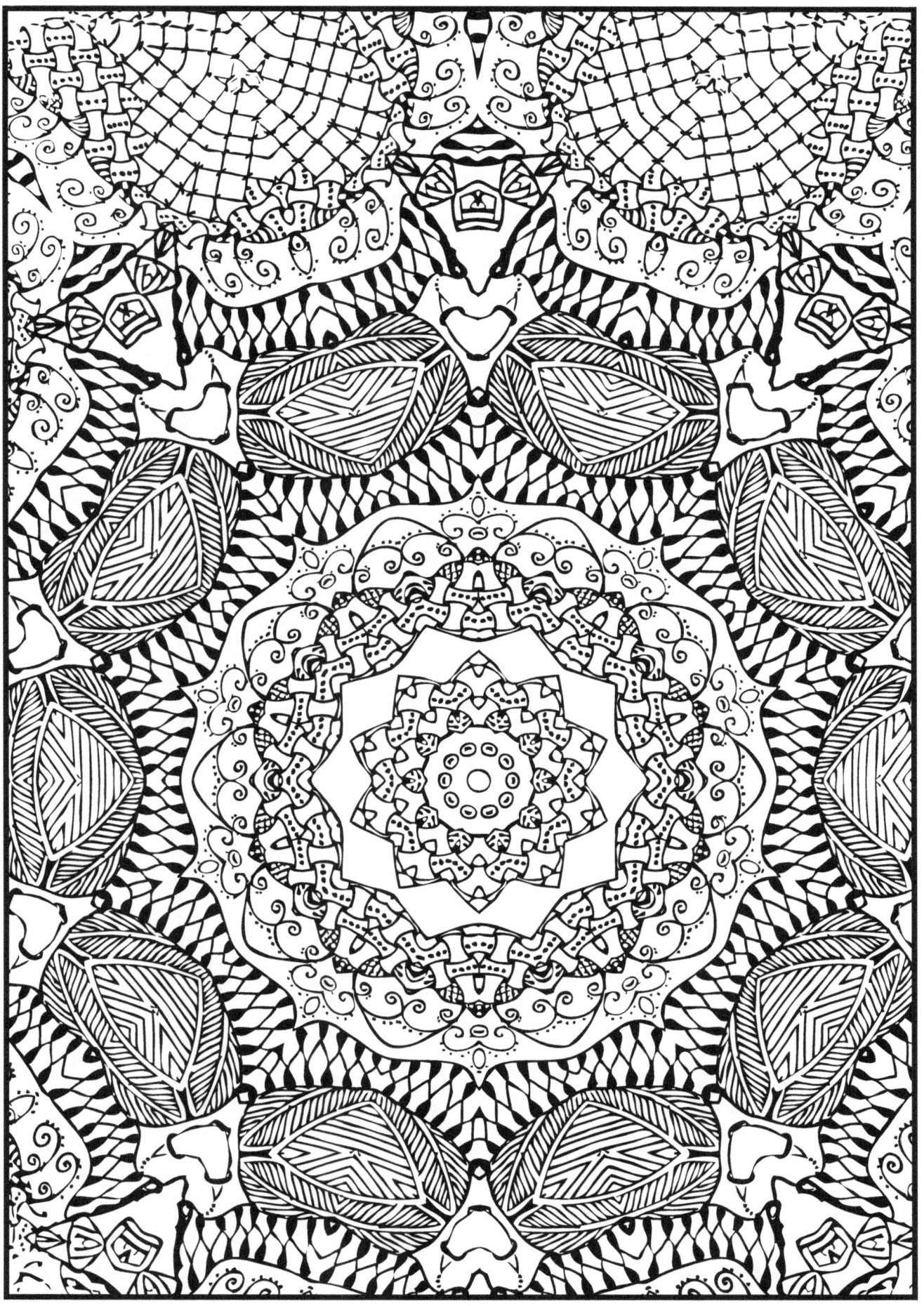

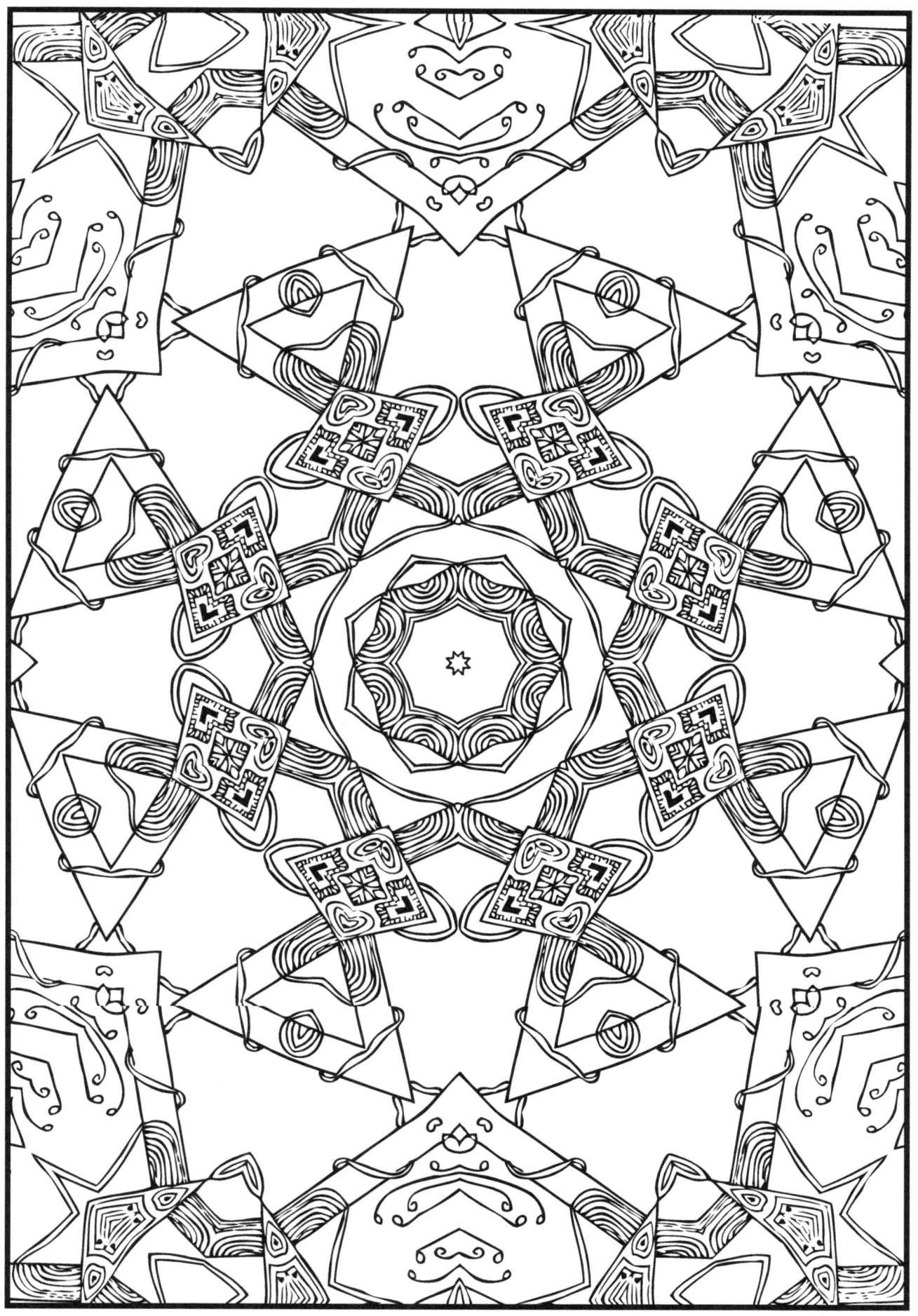

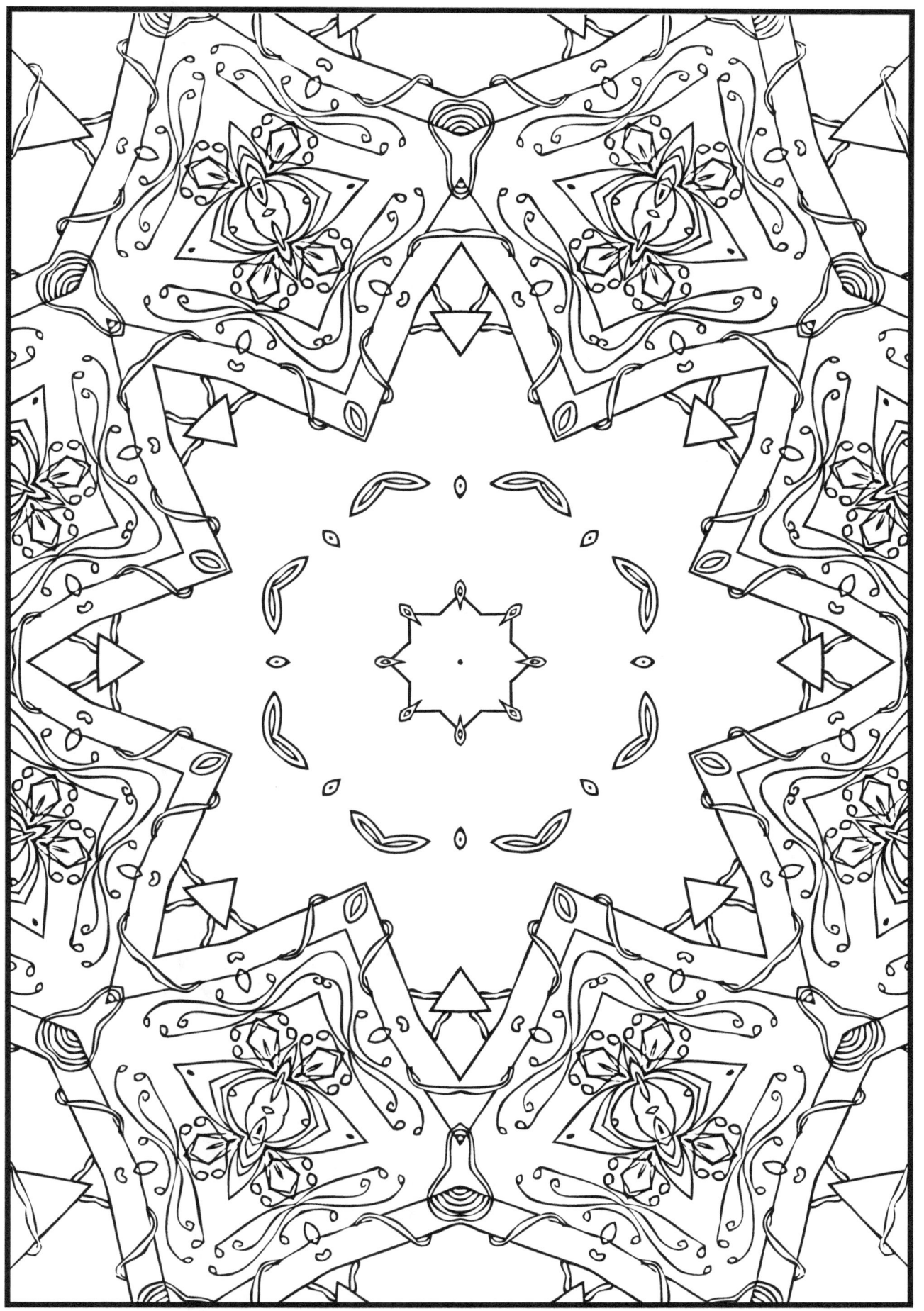

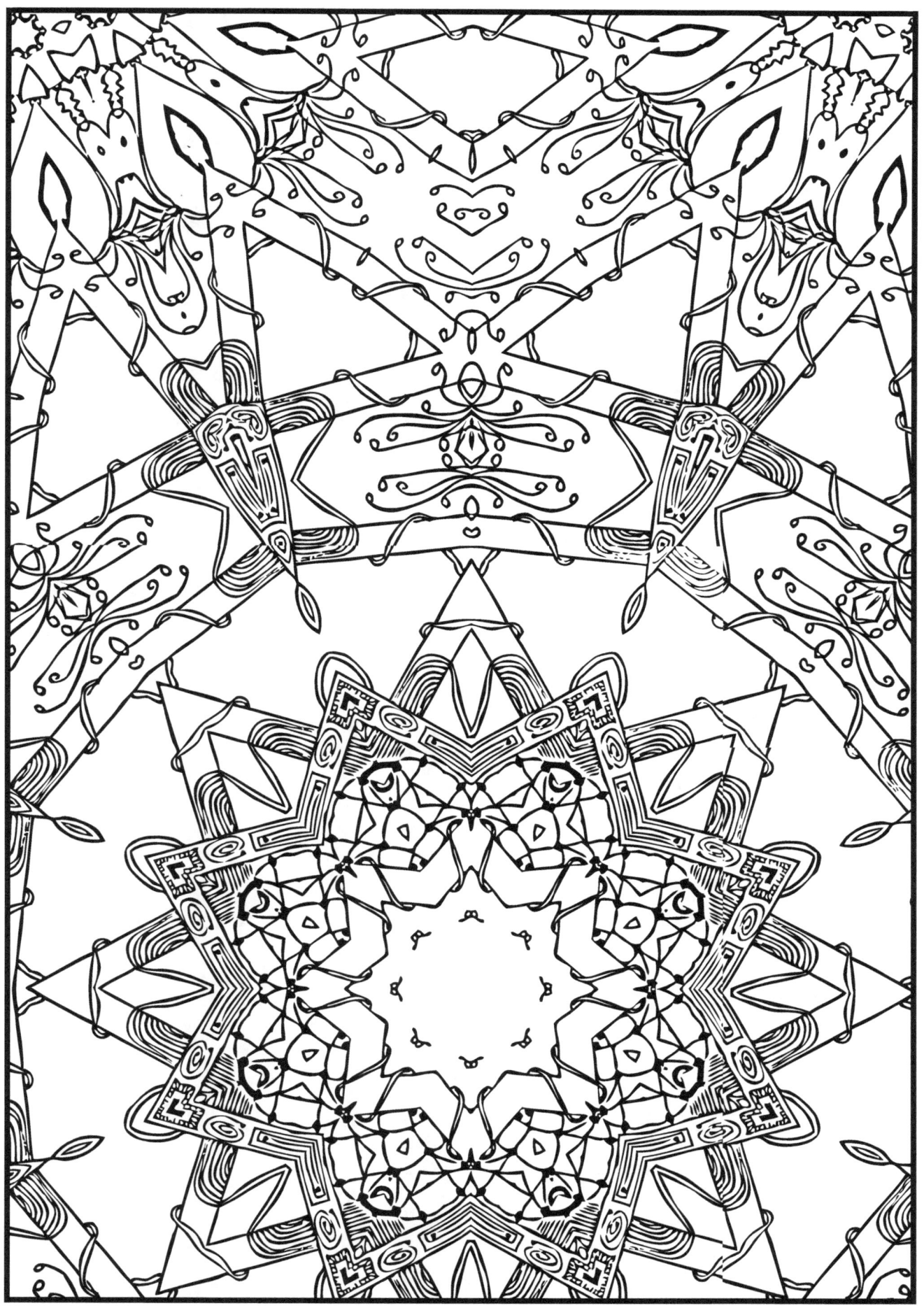

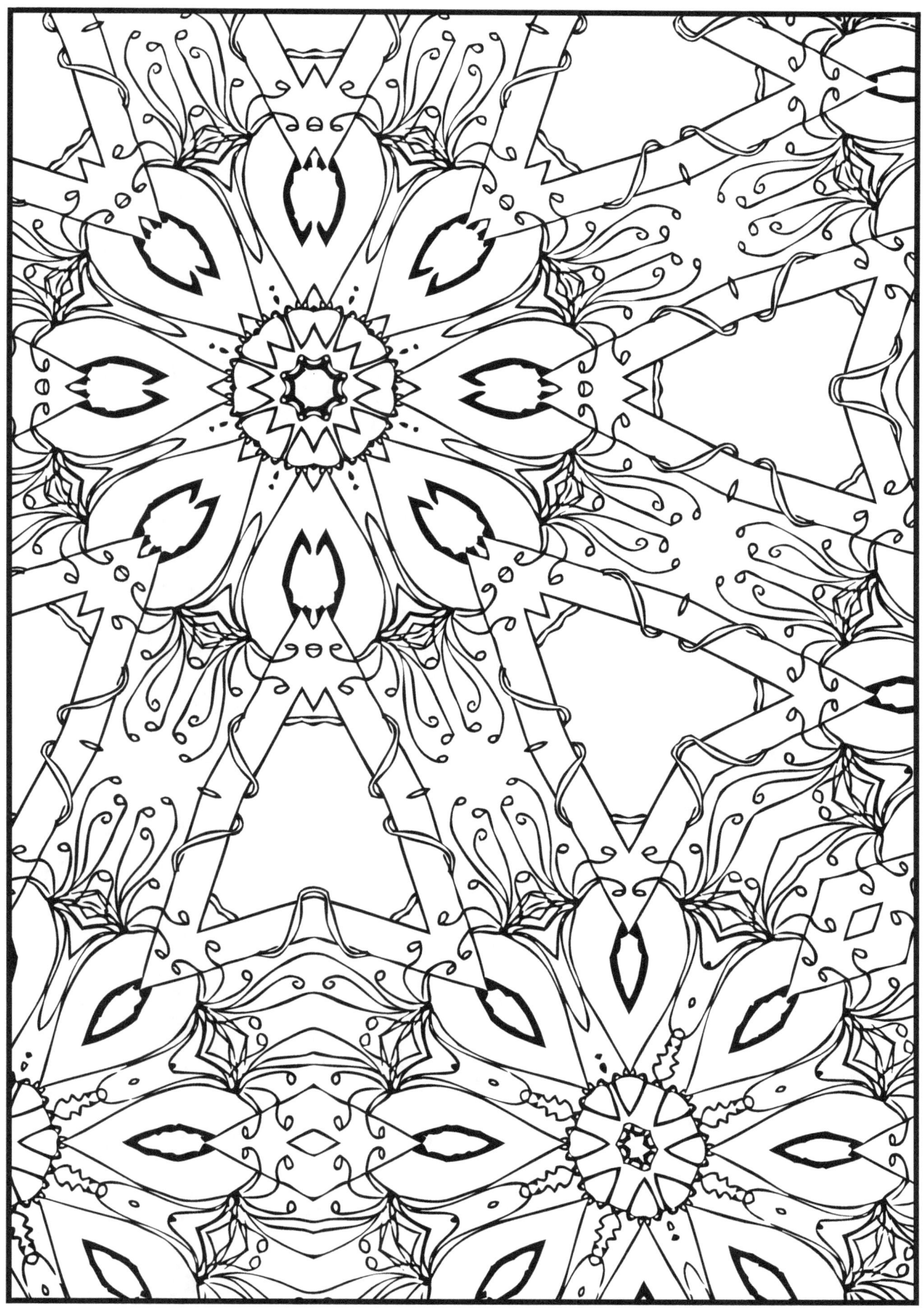

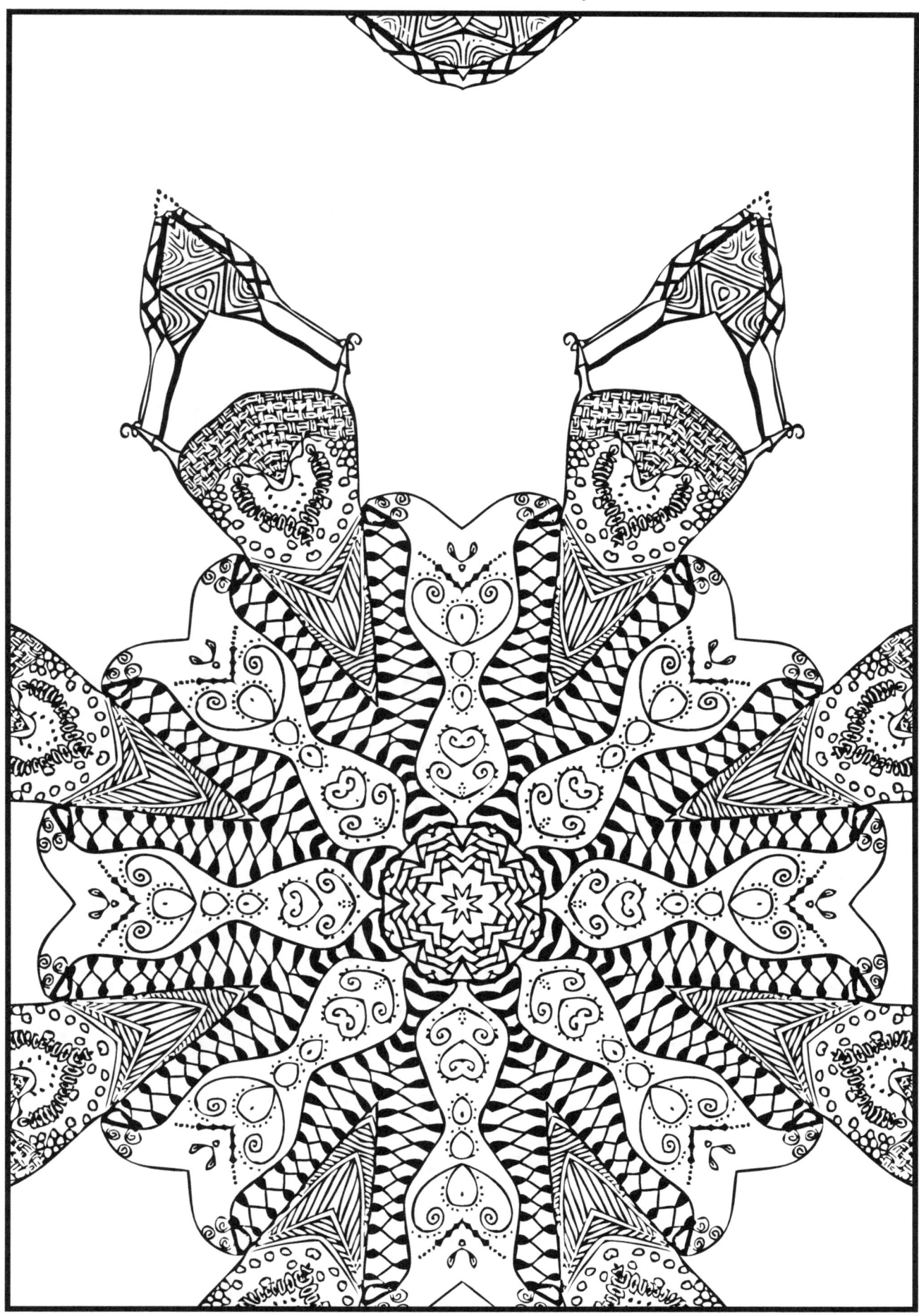

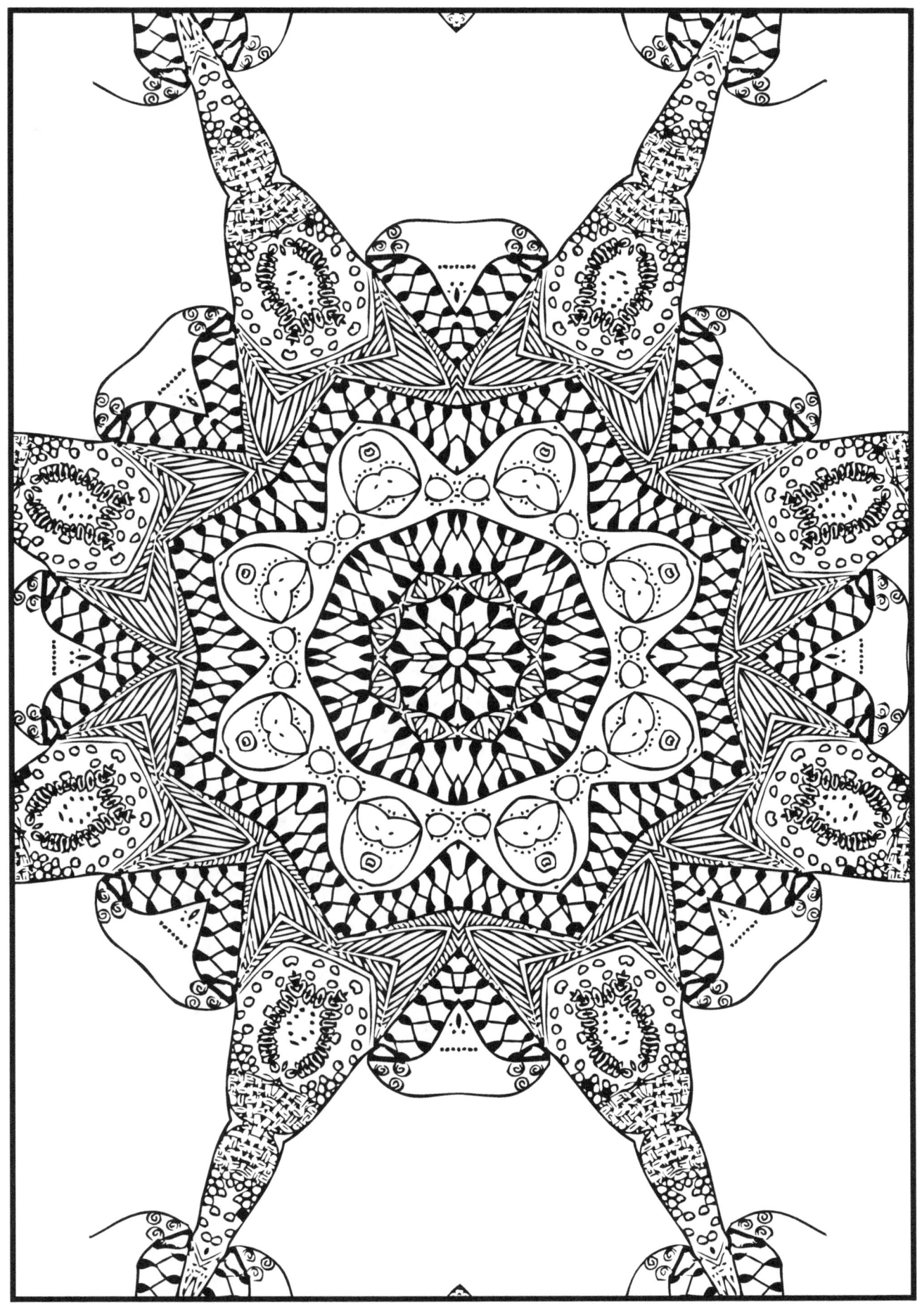

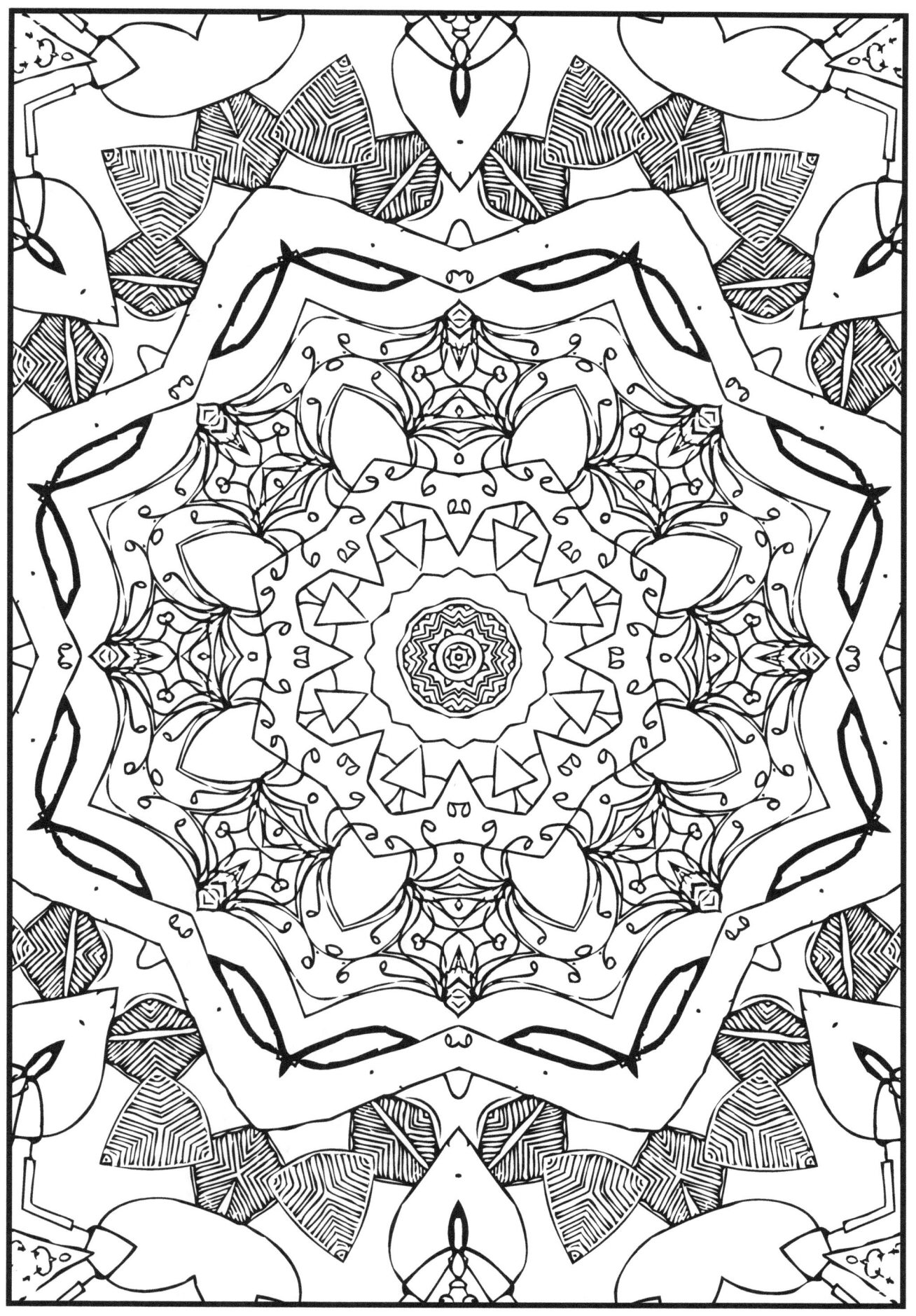

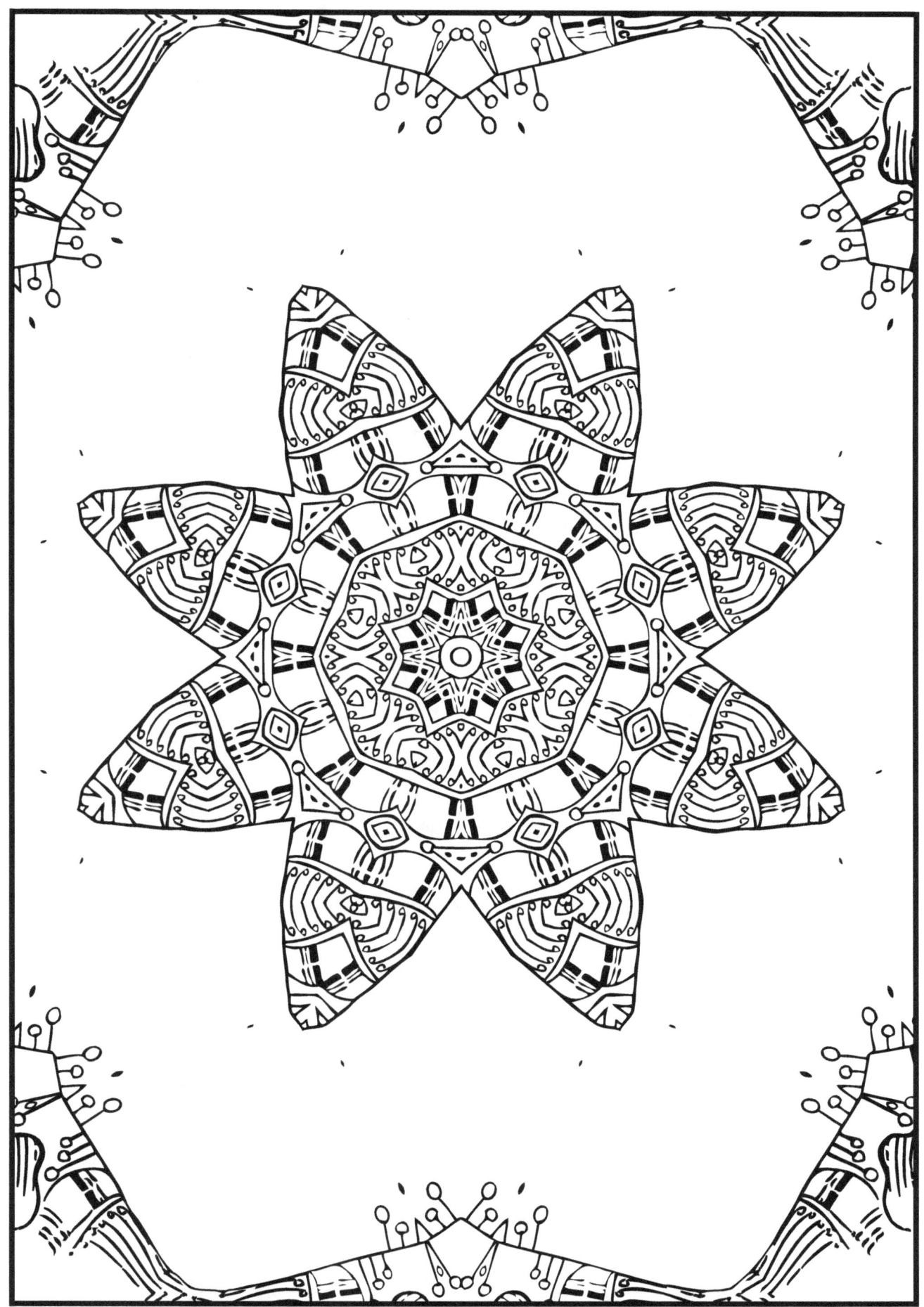

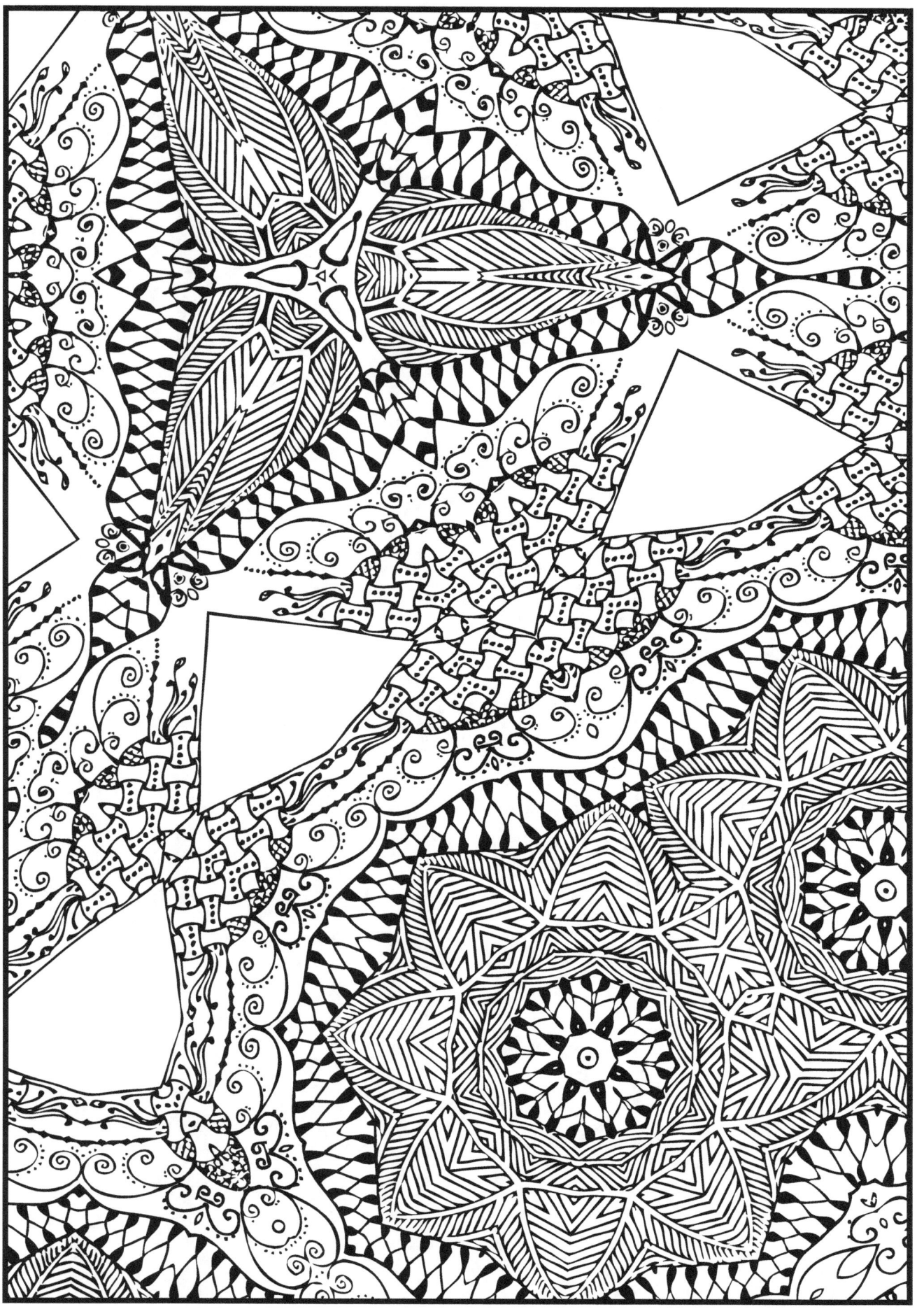

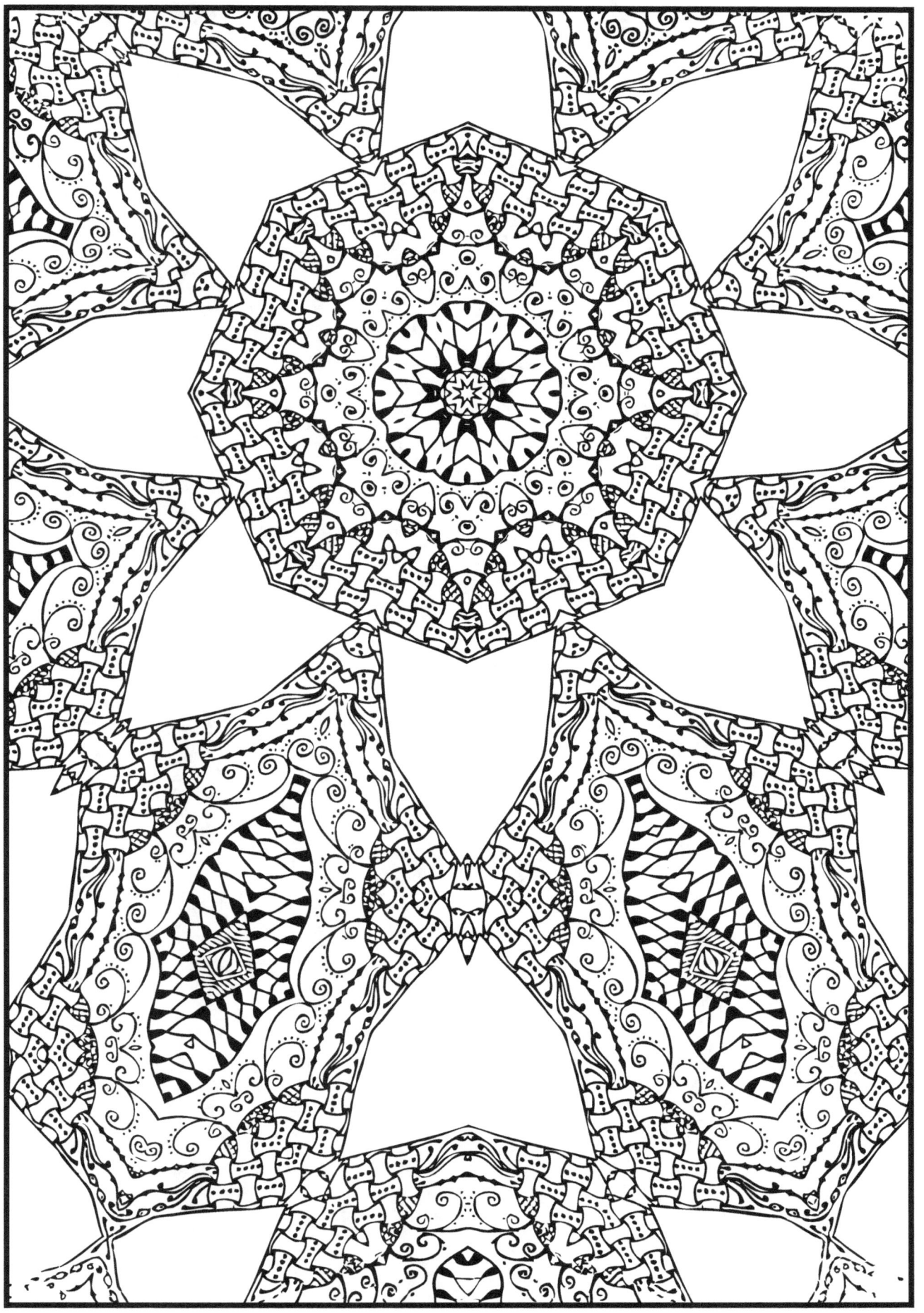

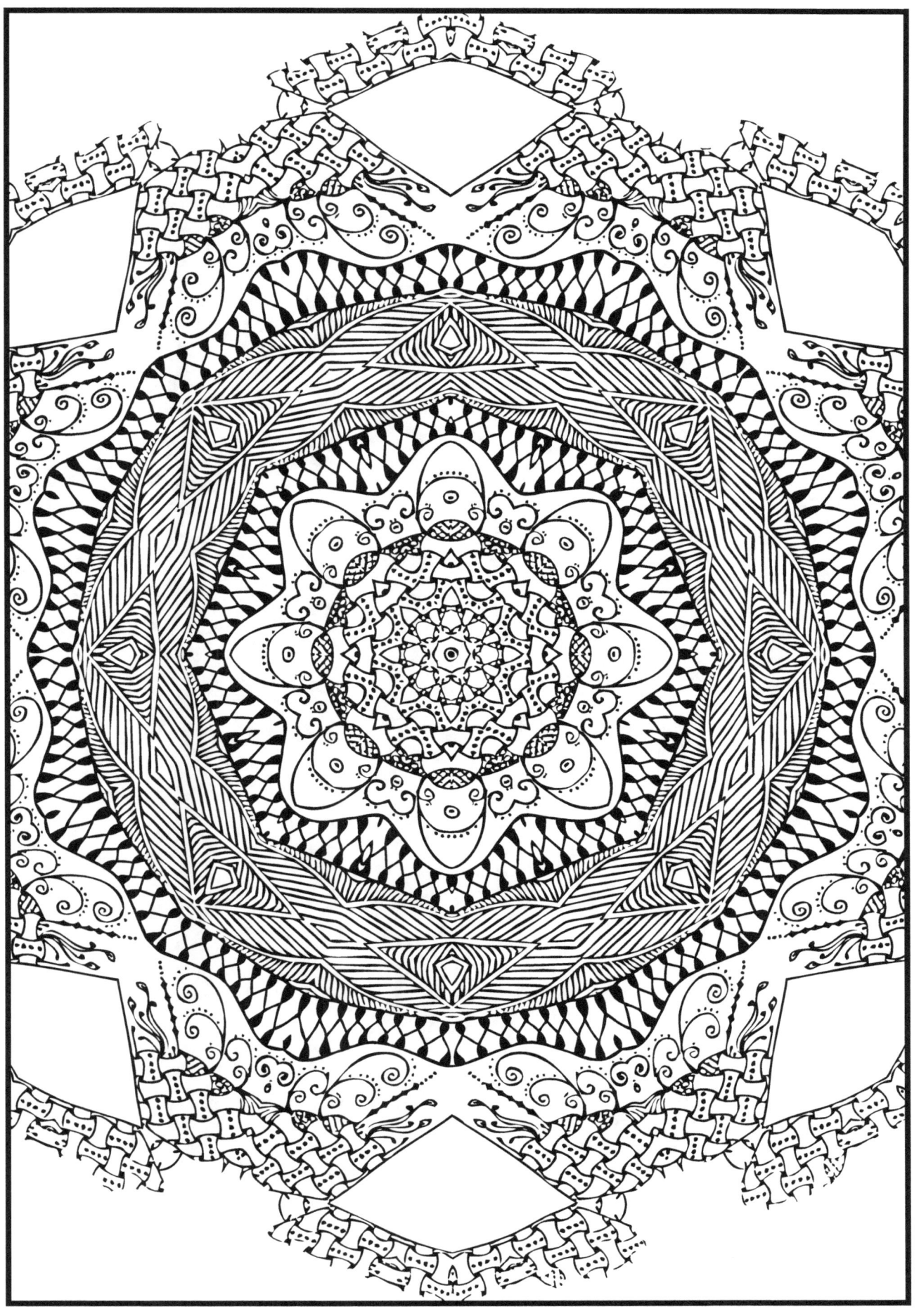

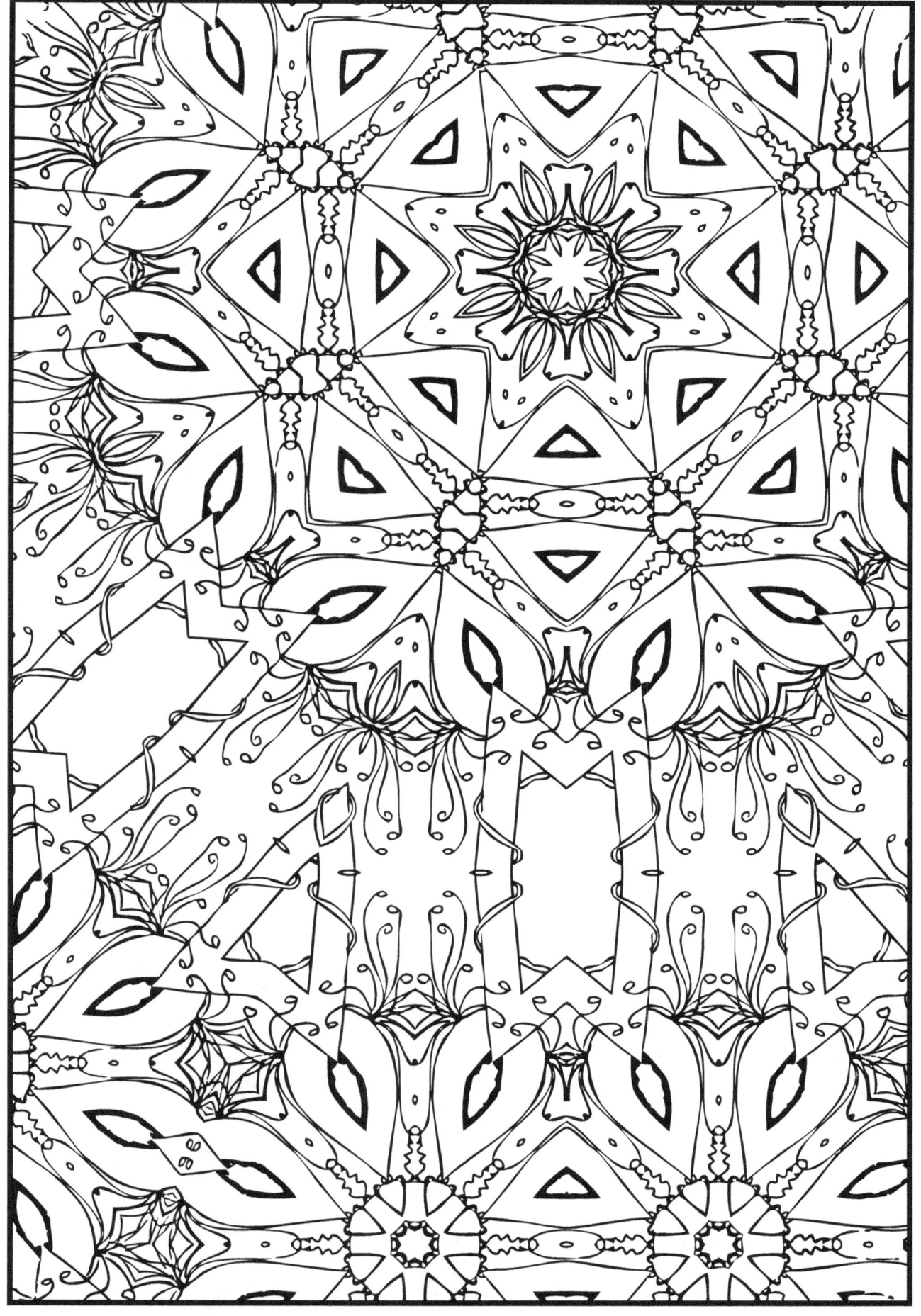

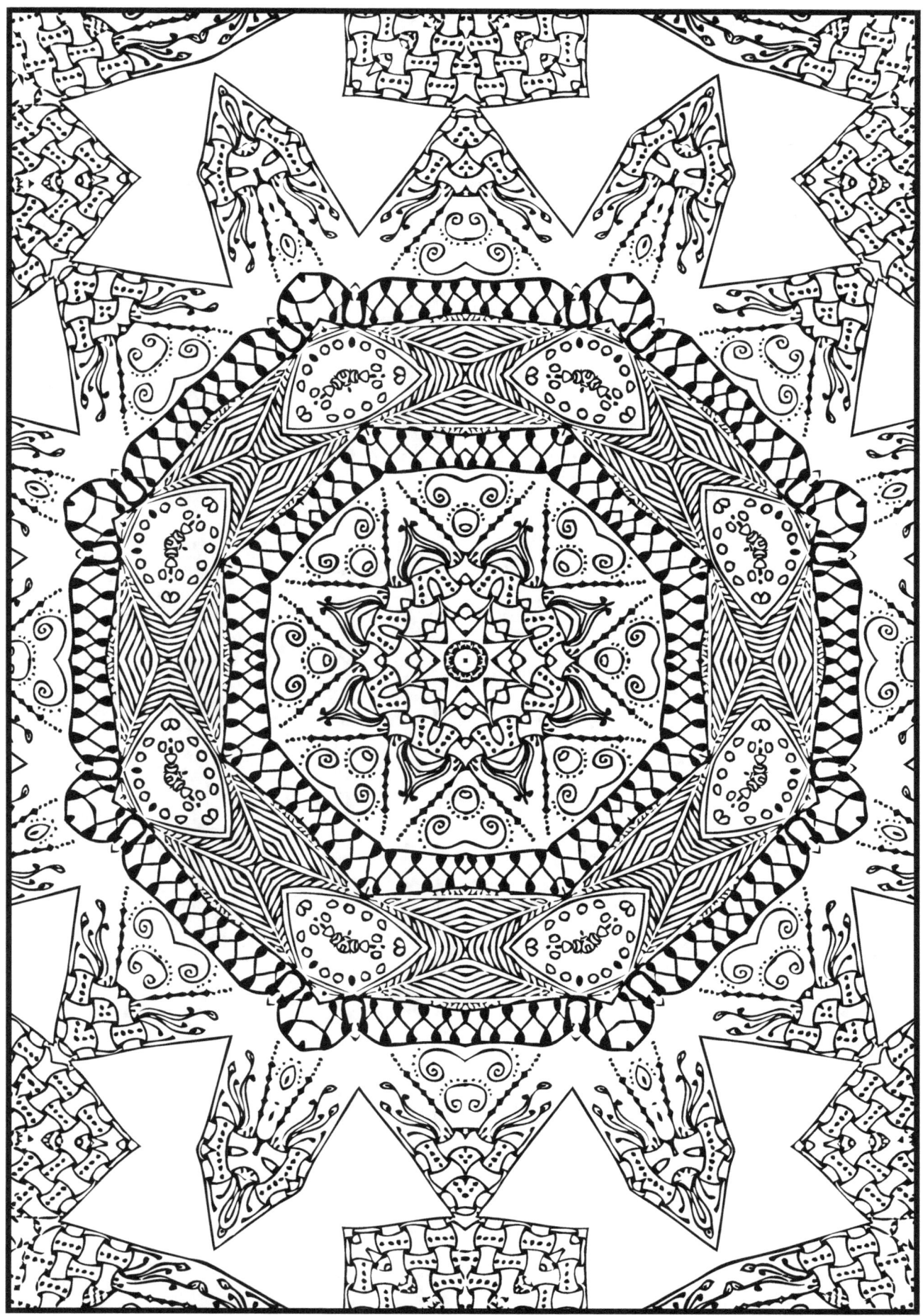

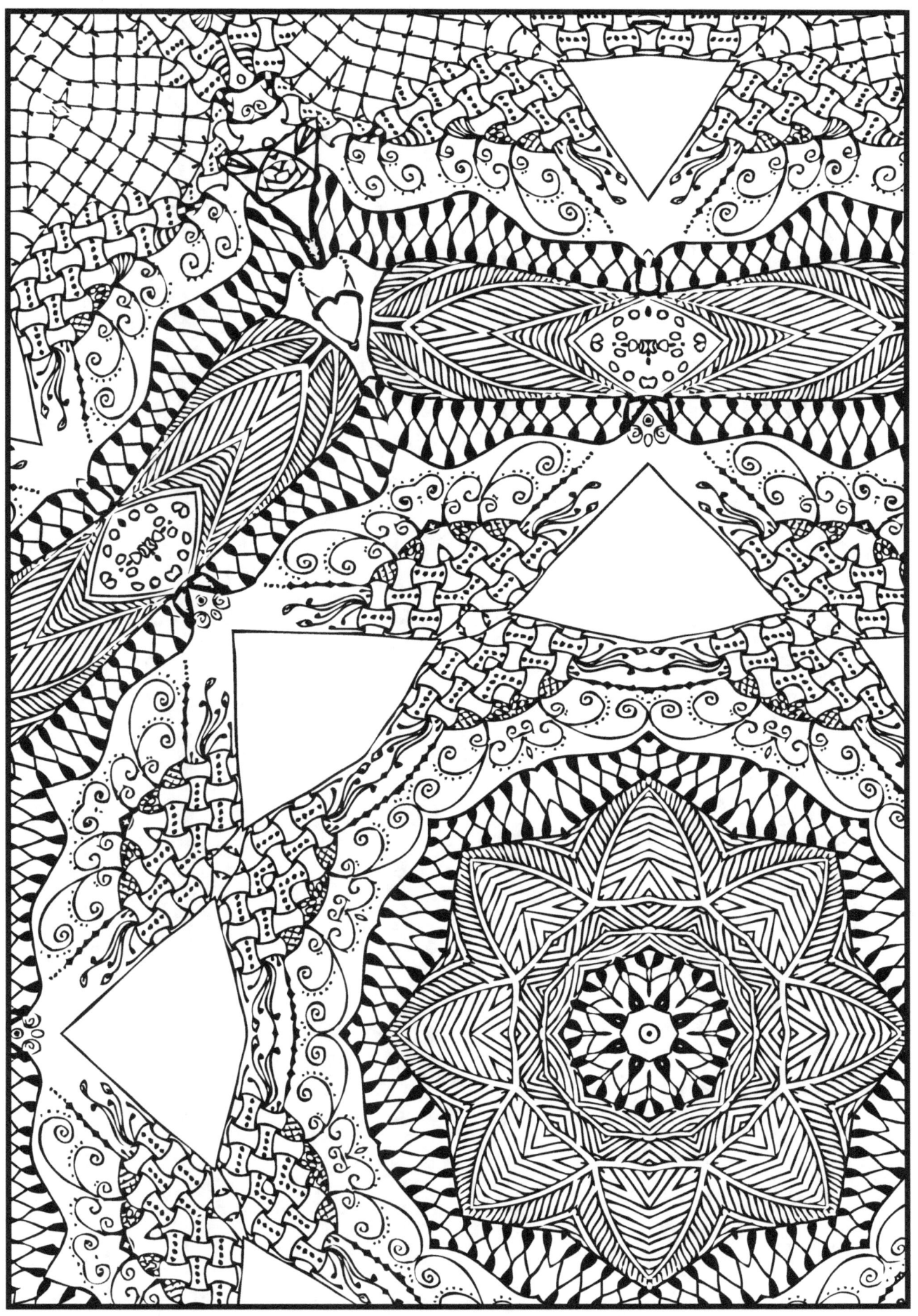

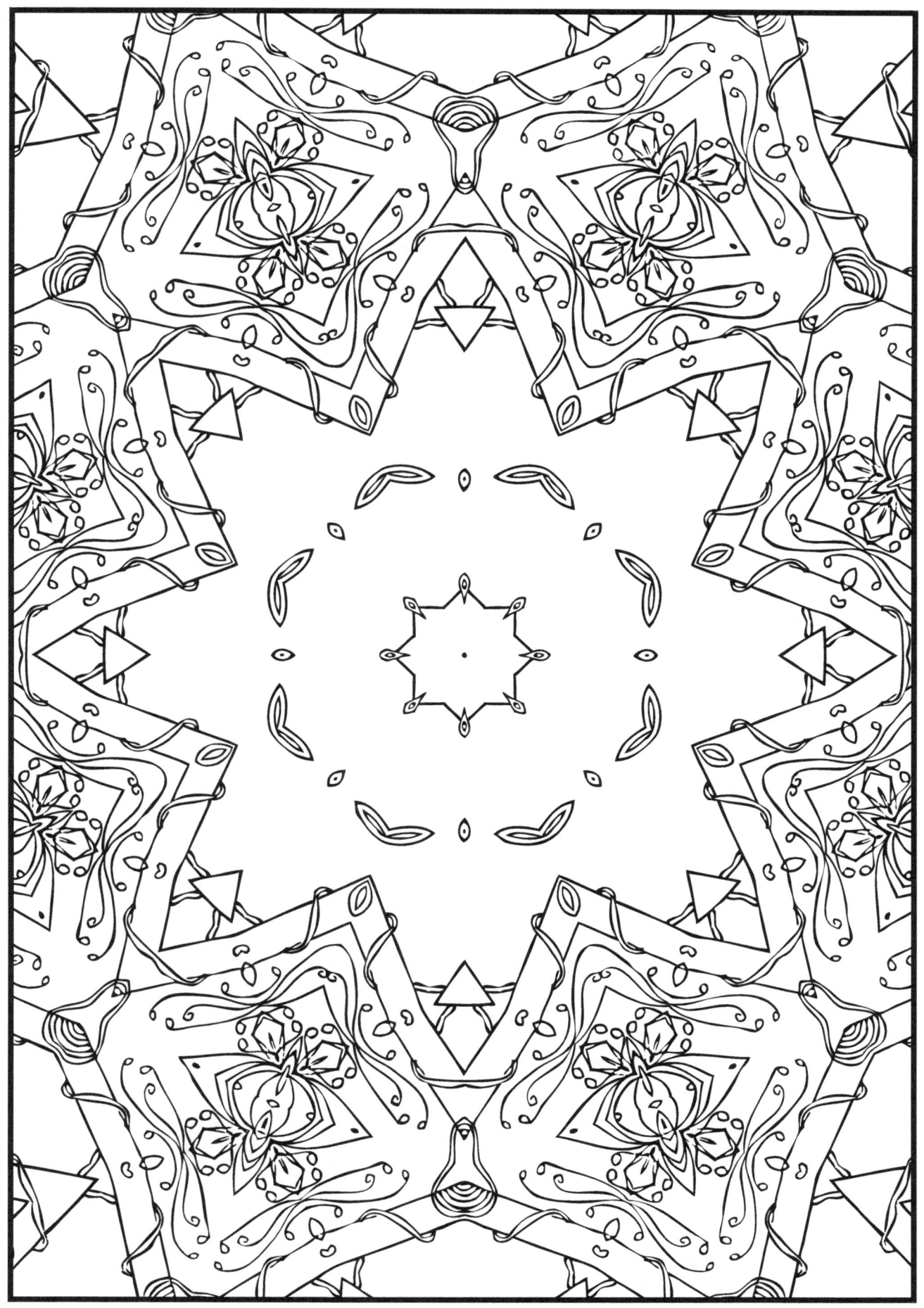

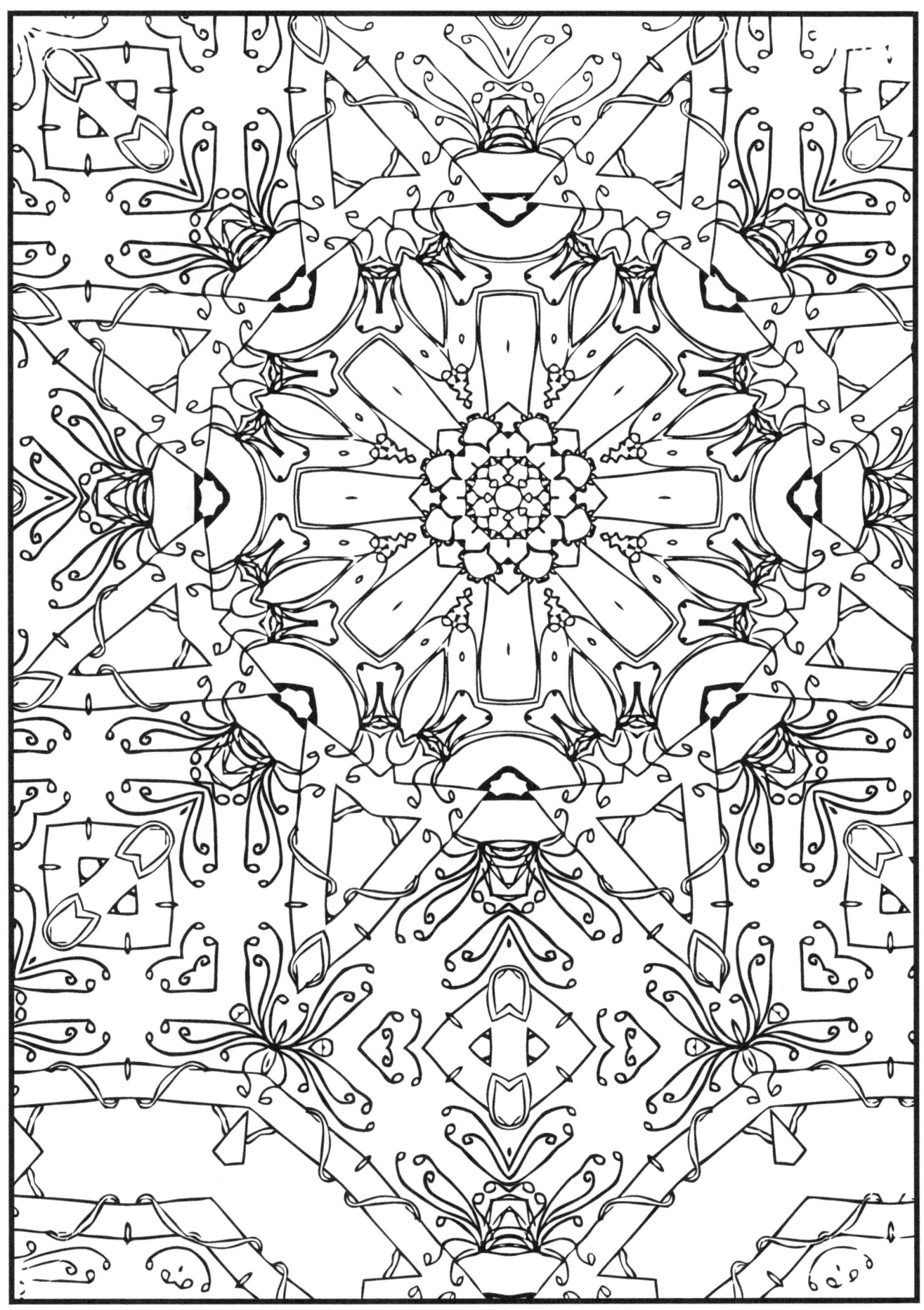

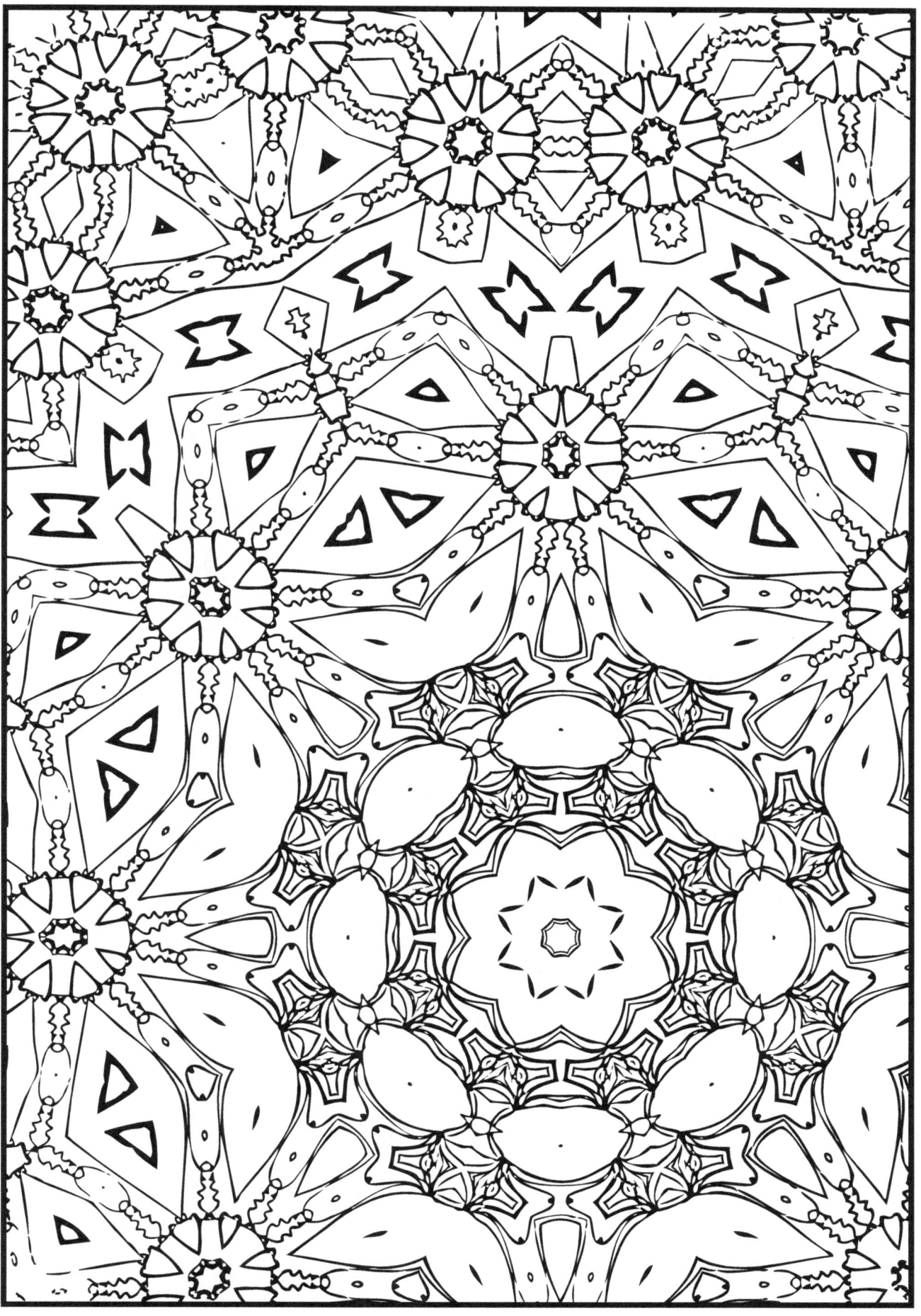

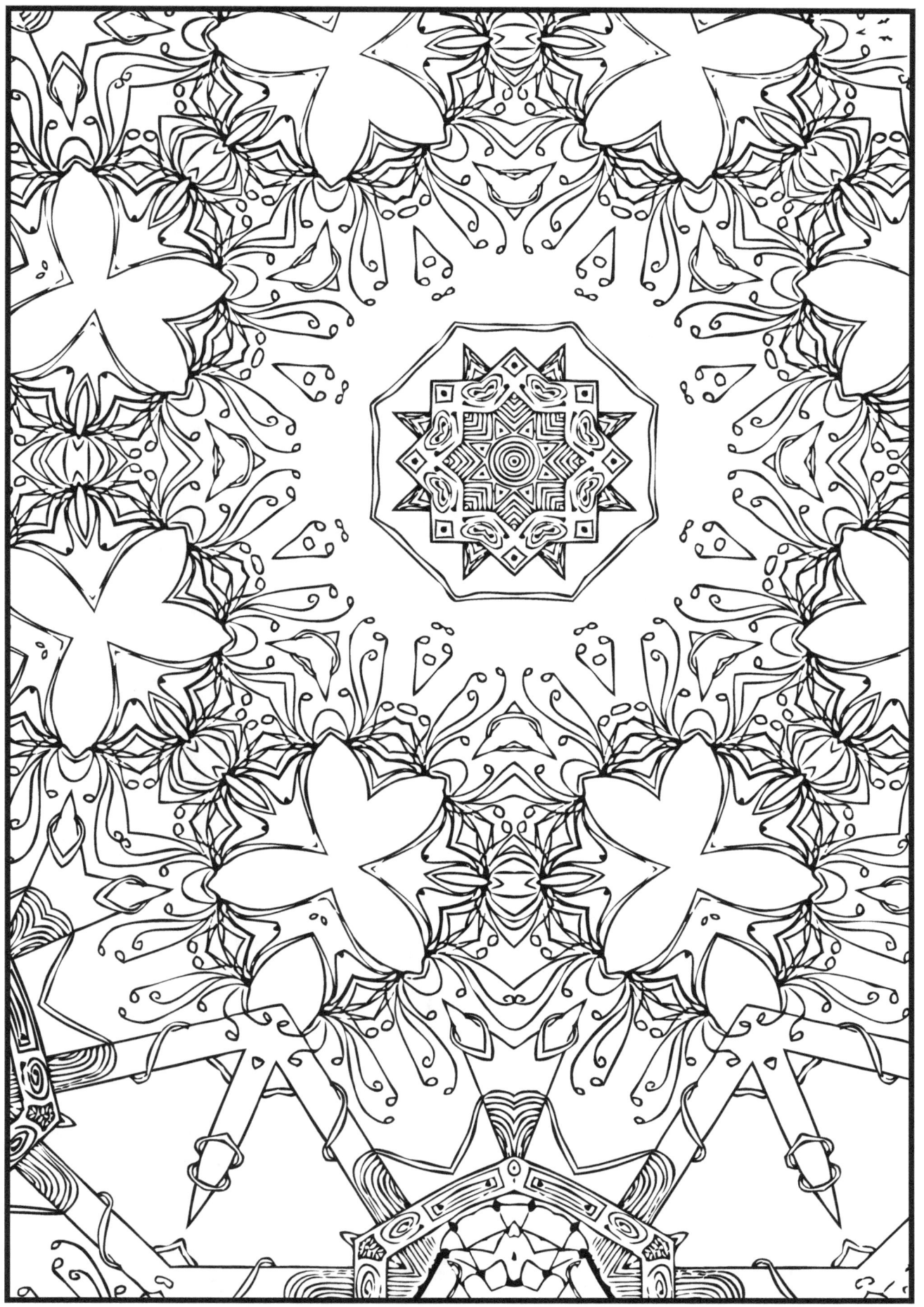

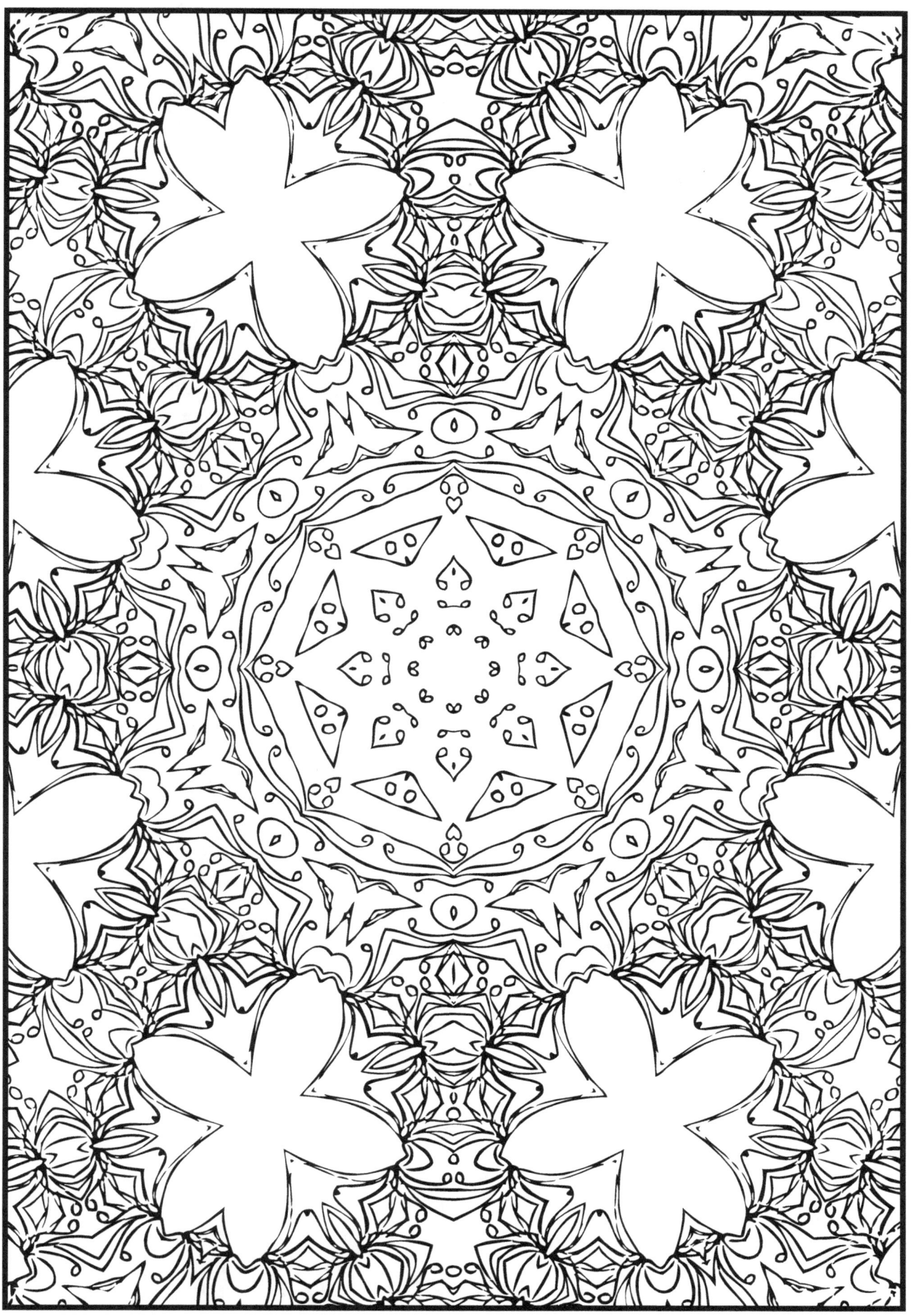

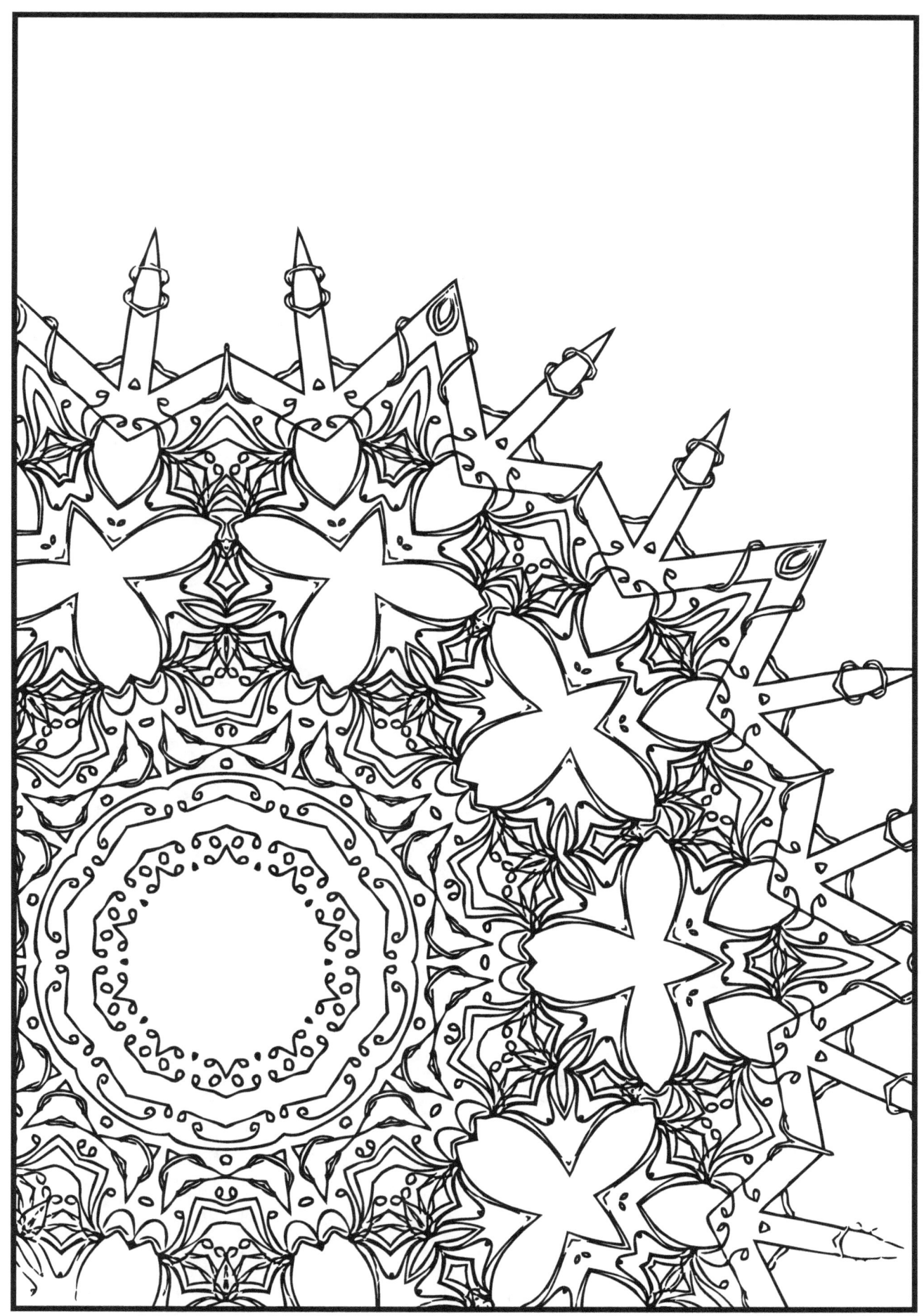

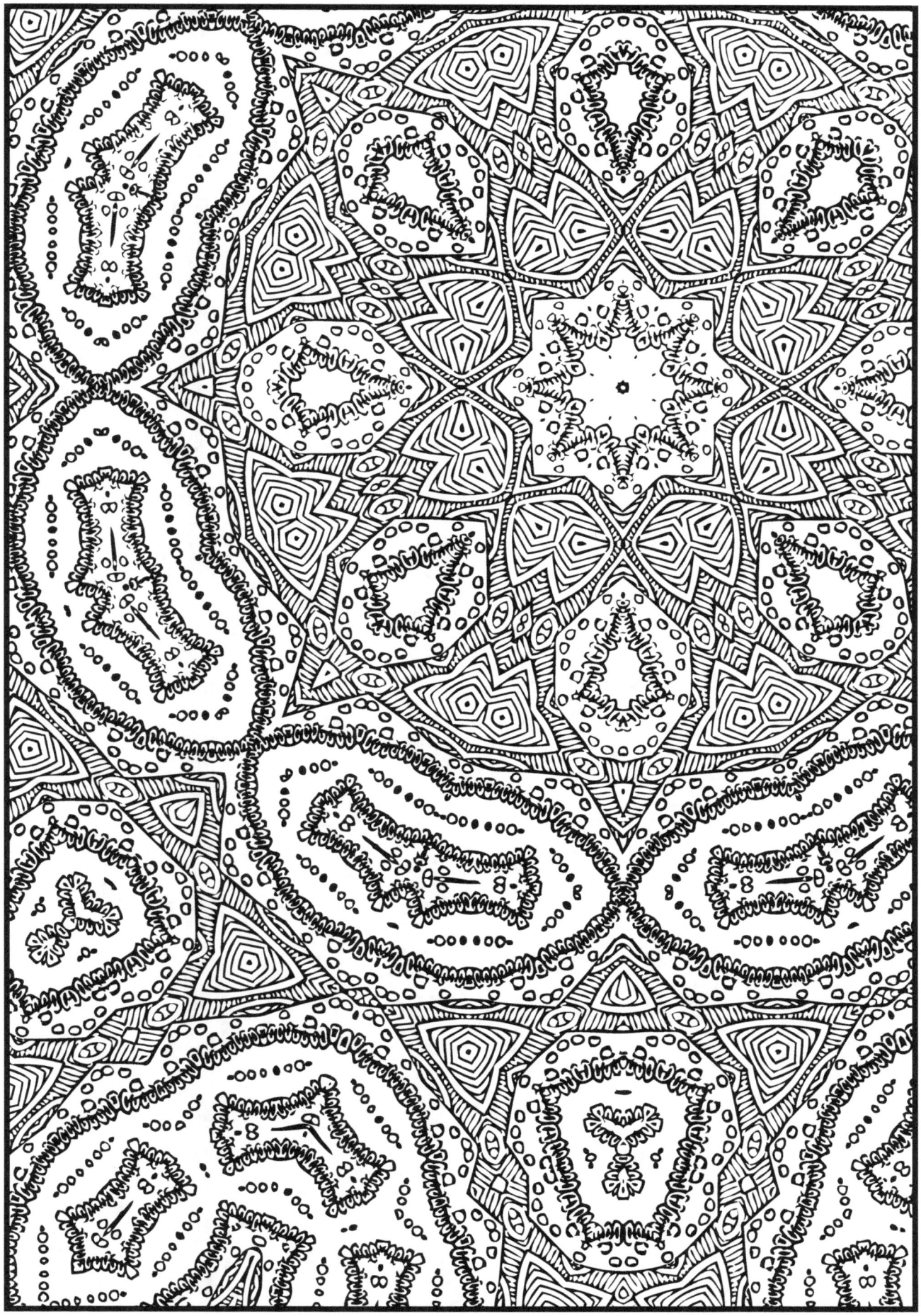

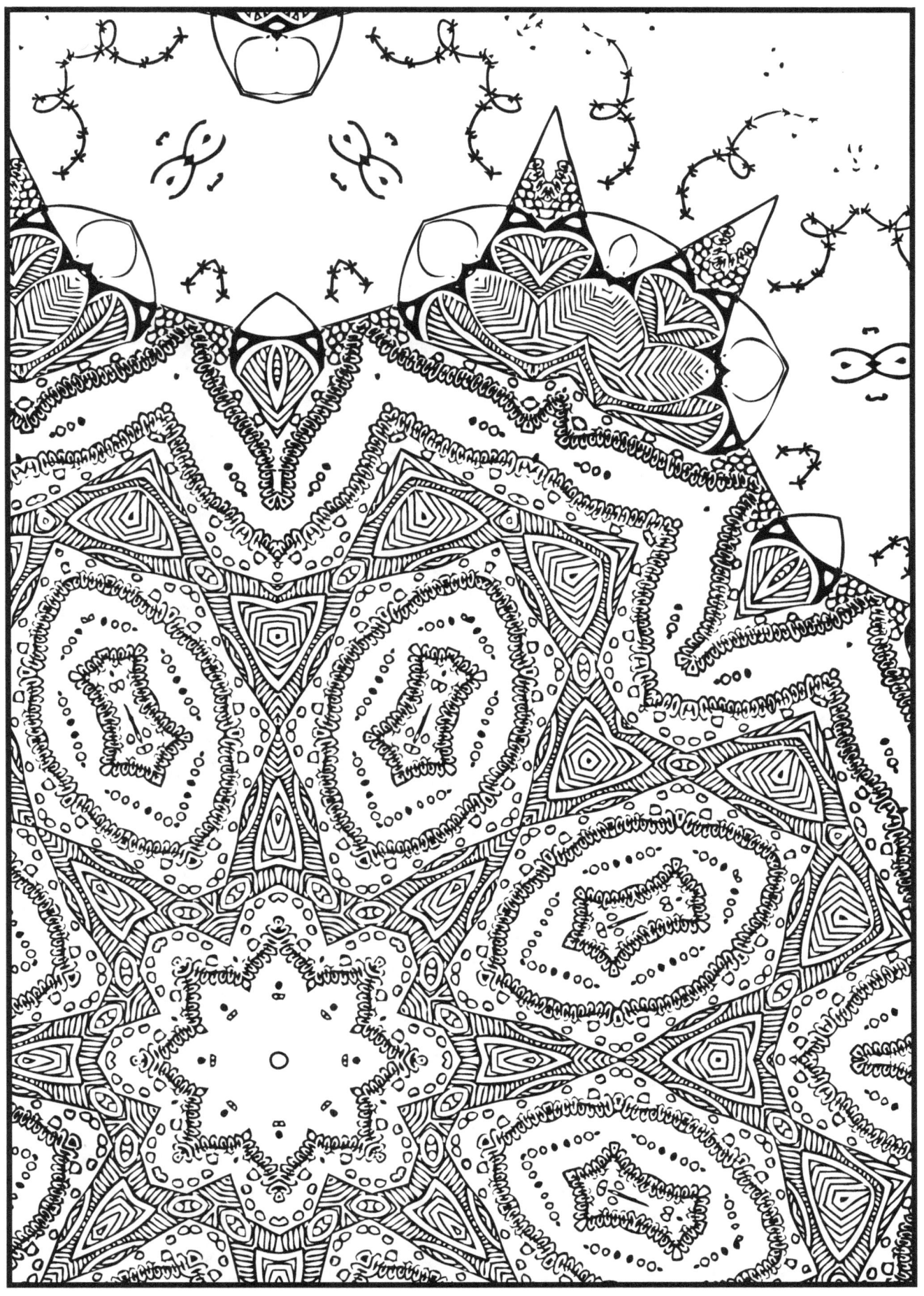

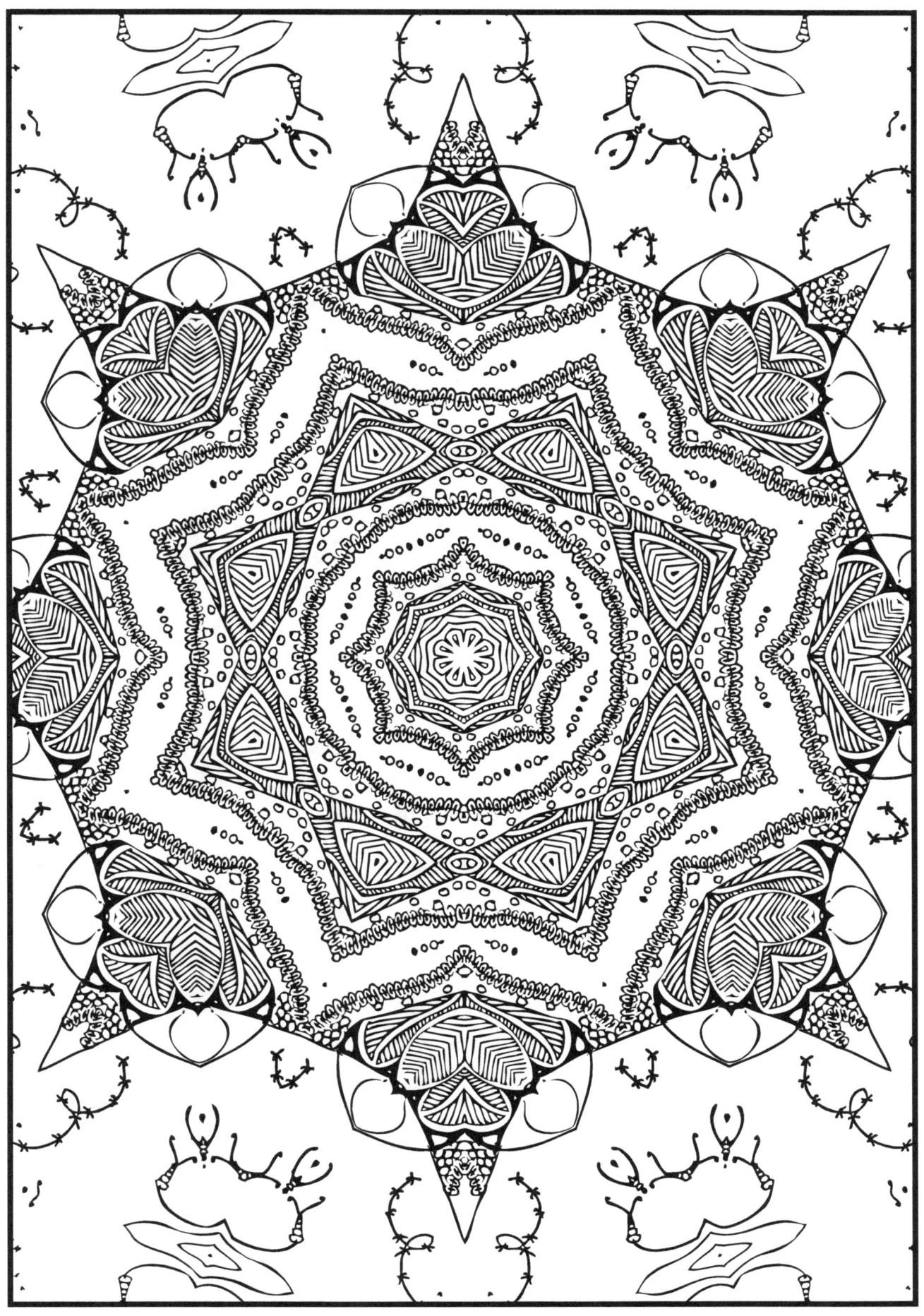

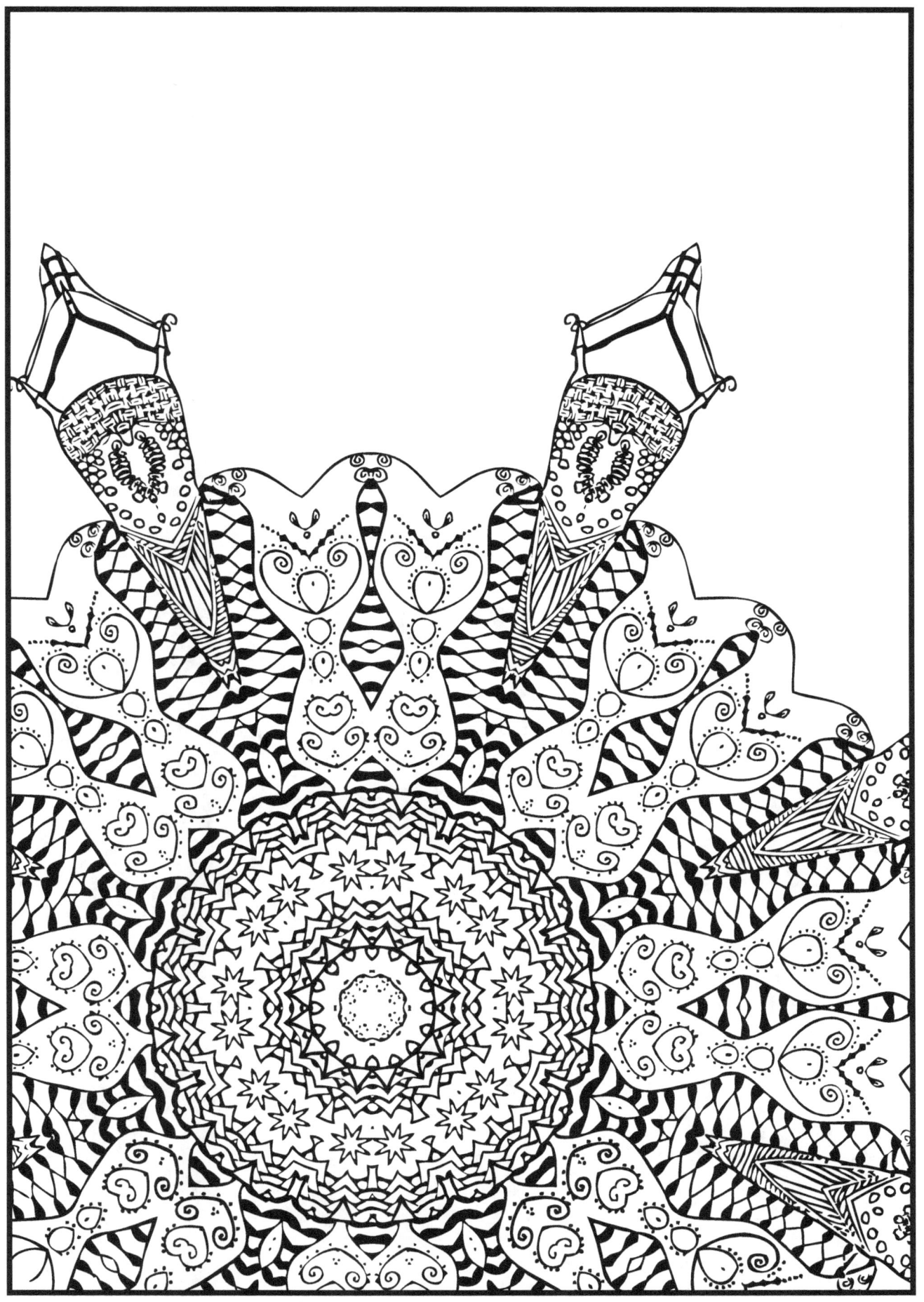

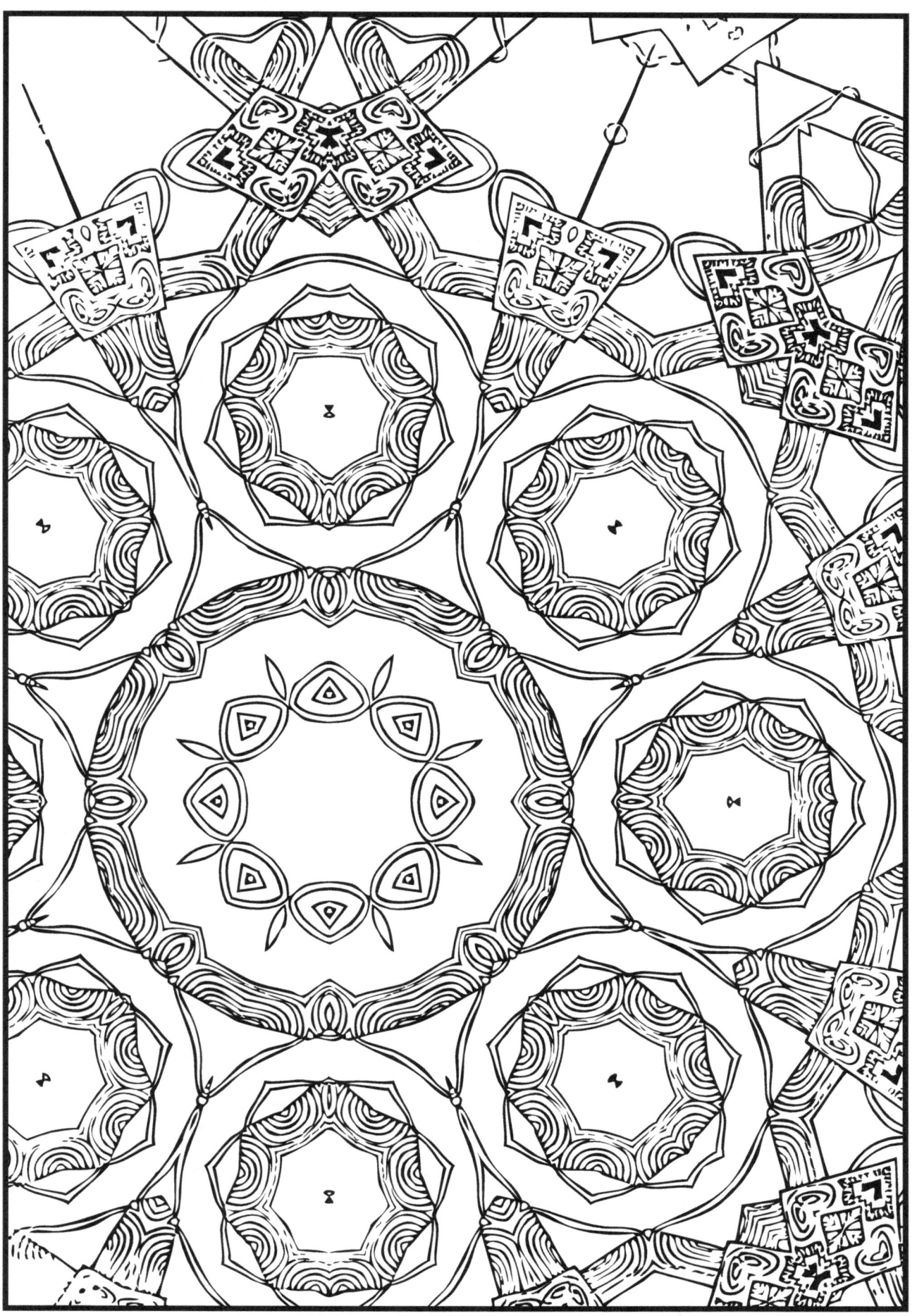

More From Andrea

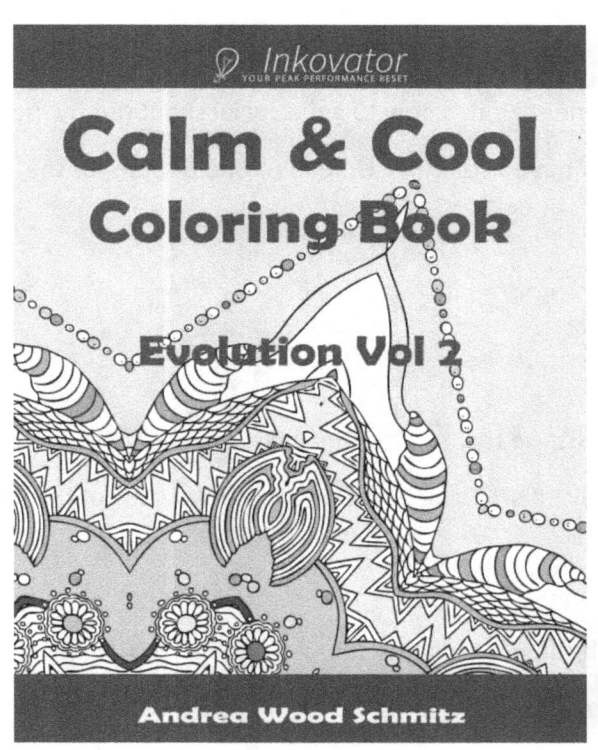

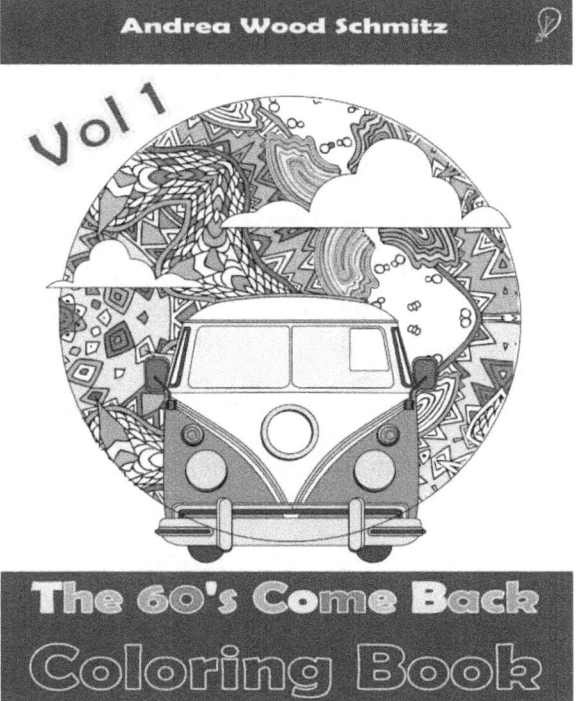

The Evolution continues with Calm & Cool, Vol 2. More whimsical, off-centered mandalas, some simple, some not, to calm you down or cool you off. Get it here: http://inkov.at/evolutionvol2

And if you like those, you'll absolutely enjoy the themed coloring books, here The 60's Come Back is filled with iconic memories of an era electric with energy, peace and love. Get it here: http://inkov.at/60vol1

For free samples from both books as well as updates for new publications, sign up at http://inkov.at/newsletter.

How else to connect with Andrea, chief Inkovator?

Follow her on Instagram: http://inkov.at/instagram

Become a fan on Facebook: http://inkov.at/facebook

Catch the growing collection of how-to-videos on Pinterest: http://inkov.at/pinterest

She's still trying to get the hang of Twitter over here: http://inkov.at/twitter

YouTube? If she starts up, then over here: http://inkov.at/youtube

Amazon author page, where you can see all books over here: http://inkov.at/amazon

Once a week I love to show off my fan's coloring. Here's how to get a social shout out by me.

First, color in a page and take a photo of it or of you coloring. Upload to one or more of the following platforms:

- Instagram
- Facebook
- Pinterest
- Twitter

Second, in your main post, where the image is, use the hashtag #inkovator so I can find it.

Third, keep your eyes peeled and every Friday I'll be giving be picking the #inkovator of the week and spreading some good cheer.

And finally, there is a private, privileged Club run by Inkovator and you are invited to join.

Join the Coloring Club run by Inkovators here: http://inkov.at/club

In the club, for a fraction of the cost of buying the books, you get access to 20 new coloring pages a month that you can download and print off as often as you want for personal coloring.

I know with 6 kids in my own house how much these get gobbled up as I've often wanted to have even my OWN copy multiple times.